The American History Series

SERIES EDITORS
John Hope Franklin, *Duke University*
Abraham S. Eisenstadt, *Brooklyn College*

Arthur S. Link
GENERAL EDITOR FOR HISTORY

Arthur S. Link
PRINCETON UNIVERSITY

Richard L. McCormick
RUTGERS UNIVERSITY

Progressivism

HARLAN DAVIDSON, INC.
WHEELING, ILLINOIS 60090-6000

Library of Congress Cataloging in Publication Data
Link, Arthur Stanley.
    Progressivism

    (The American history series)
    Bibliography: p. 119
    Includes index.
    1. Progressivism (United States politics) 2. United States—Politics and
government—1865–1933.   I. McCormick, Richard L.   II. Title.   III. Series:
American history series (Harlan Davidson, Inc.)
E743.L56   1983   322.4'4'0973   82-15857
ISBN 0-88295-814-3

Cover design: Roger Eggers. Cover illustration: A "Tipple Boy" at the
Turkey Knob Mine in MacDonald, West Virginia. Photograph by Lewis
Hine, 1908. Library of Congress.

Manufactured in the United States of America
97 9 10 11 MG

FOREWORD

Every generation writes its own history, for the reason that it sees the past in the foreshortened perspective of its own experience. This has certainly been true of the writing of American history. The practical aim of our historiography is to offer us a more certain sense of where we are going by helping us understand the road we took in getting where we are. If the substance and nature of our historical writing is changing, it is precisely because our own generation is redefining its direction, much as the generations that preceded us redefined theirs. We are seeking a newer direction, because we are facing new problems, changing our values and premises, and shaping new institutions to meet new needs. Thus, the vitality of the present inspires the vitality of our writing about our past. Today's scholars are hard at work reconsidering every major field of our history: its politics, diplomacy, economy, society, mores, values, sexuality, and status, ethnic, and race relations. No less significantly, our scholars are using newer modes of investigation to probe the ever-expanding domain of the American past.

Our aim, in this American History Series, is to offer the reader a survey of what scholars are saying about the central themes and issues of American history. To present these themes and issues, we have invited scholars who have made notable contributions to the respective fields in which they are writing. Each volume offers the reader a sufficient factual and narrative account for perceiving the larger dimensions of its particular subject. Addressing their respective themes, our authors have undertaken, moreover, to present the conclusions derived by the principal writers on these themes. Beyond that, the authors present their own conclusions about those aspects of their respective subjects that have been matters of difference and controversy. In effect, they have written not only about where the subject stands in today's historiography but also about where they stand on their subject. Each volume closes with an extensive critical essay on the writings of the major authorities on its particular theme.

The books in this series are designed for use in both basic and advanced courses in American history. Such a series has a particular utility in times such as these, when the traditional format of our American history courses is being altered to accommodate a greater diversity of texts and reading materials. The series offers a number of distinct advantages. It extends and deepens the dimensions of course work in American history. In proceeding beyond the confines of the traditional textbook, it makes clear that the study of our past is, more than the student might otherwise infer, at once complex, sophisticated, and profound. It presents American history as a subject of continuing vitality and fresh investigation. The work of experts in their respective fields, it opens up to the student the rich findings of historical inquiry. It invites the student to join, in major fields of research, the many groups of scholars who are pondering anew the central themes and problems of our past. It challenges the student to participate actively in exploring American history and to collaborate in the creative and rigorous adventure of seeking out its wider reaches.

John Hope Franklin

Abraham S. Eisenstadt

ACKNOWLEDGMENTS

We are grateful to a number of persons for their generous help to us at various stages in the writing of this book. The editors of this series, John Hope Franklin and Abraham S. Eisenstadt, encouraged us from the beginning of this project and suggested numerous wise revisions. Paula Baker, Paul G. E. Clemens, Suzanne Lebsock, James Reed, and William A. Link read and commented upon all or parts of the manuscript in its earlier drafts. Lewis L. Gould, who served as an outside reader for our publisher, provided a detailed and helpful critique. William H. Harbaugh read the entire work with care just prior to our final revisions and made several useful suggestions. Denise Thompson typed the final manuscript with great care; Roberta Clemens did a thorough, meticulous reading of the proofs. Maureen Gilgore Trobec, the managing editor of Harlan Davidson, Inc., edited our manuscript with sensitivity and gracefulness. Finally, without the suggestion and prompting of our publisher, Harlan Davidson, this book would never have been written at all. We thank sincerely all these friends and colleagues. However, we alone are responsible for whatever defects this book has.

Arthur S. Link

Richard L. McCormick

CONTENTS

ONE

Progressivism in History

Convulsive reform movements swept across the American landscape from the 1890s to 1917. Angry farmers demanded better prices for their products, regulation of the railroads, and the destruction of what they thought was the evil power of bankers, middlemen, and corrupt politicians. Urban residents crusaded for better city services and more efficient municipal government. Members of various professions, such as social workers and doctors, tried to improve the dangerous and unhealthy conditions in which many people lived and worked.

Businessmen, too, lobbied incessantly for goals which they defined as reform. Never before had the people of the United States engaged in so many diverse movements for the improvement of their political system, economy, and communities. By around 1910, many of these crusading men and women were calling themselves progressives. Ever since, historians have used the term *progressivism* to describe the many reform movements of the early twentieth century.

Yet in the goals they sought and the remedies they tried, the reformers were a varied and contradictory lot. Some progressives wanted to increase the political influence and control of ordinary people, while other progressives wanted to concentrate authority in experts. Many reformers tried to curtail the growth of large corporations; others accepted bigness in industry on account of its supposed economic benefits. Some progressives were genuinely concerned about the welfare of the "new" immigrants from southern and eastern Europe; other progressives sought, sometimes frantically, to "Americanize" the newcomers or to keep them out altogether. In general, progressives sought to improve the conditions of life and labor and to create as much social stability as possible. But each group of progressives had its own definitions of improvement and stability. In the face of such diversity, one historian, Peter G. Filene, has even argued that what has been called the progressive movement never existed as a historical phenomenon ("An Obituary for 'The Progressive Movement,'" *American Quarterly,* 1970).

Certainly there was no *unified* movement, but, like most students of the period, we consider progressivism to have been a real, vital, and significant phenomenon, one which contemporaries recognized and talked and fought about. Properly conceptualized, progressivism provides a useful framework for the history of the United States in the late nineteenth and early twentieth centuries.

One source of confusion and controversy about progressives and progressivism is the words themselves. They are often used judgmentally to describe people and changes which historians have deemed to be "good," "enlightened," and "farsighted." The progressives themselves naturally intended the words to convey such positive qualities, but we should not accept their usage uncritically. It might be better to avoid the terms progressive and progressivism altogether, but they are too deeply embedded in the language of contemporaries and historians to be ignored. Besides, we think that the terms have real meaning. In this book the words will be used neutrally, without any implicit judgment about the value of reform.

In the broadest sense, progressivism was the way in which a whole generation of Americans defined themselves politically and responded to the nation's problems at the turn of the century. The progressives made the first comprehensive efforts to grapple with the ills of a modern urban-industrial society. Hence the record of their achievements and failures has considerable relevance for our own time.

WHO WERE THE PROGRESSIVES?

Ever since the early twentieth century, people have argued about who the progressives were and what they stood for. This may seem to be a strange topic of debate, but it really is not. Progressivism engaged many different groups of Americans, and each group of progressives naturally considered themselves to be the key reformers and thought that their own programs were the most important ones. Not surprisingly, historians ever since have had trouble agreeing on who really shaped progressivism and its goals. Scholars who have written about the period have variously identified farmers, the old middle classes, professionals, businessmen, and urban immigrants and ethnic groups as the core group of progressives. But these historians have succeeded in identifying *their* reformers only by defining progressivism narrowly, by excluding other reformers and reforms when they do not fall within some specific definition, and by resorting to such vague, catch-all adjectives as "middle class." Who, then, were the progressives?

To many of the reformers themselves, and to the earliest

historians of the progressive period, the answer to this question was simple and clear: common people—farmers, workers, and small businessmen—organized the progressive movement in order to recapture power from the railroads, large corporations, and party bosses who had plundered the United States during the Gilded Age. Benjamin Parke DeWitt gave the classic statement of this viewpoint in *The Progressive Movement* (1915); it was echoed in more analytical, but equally sympathetic, works written in the 1920s and 1930s by Charles A. and Mary R. Beard, Vernon Louis Parrington, and Harold U. Faulkner. In their view, progressivism was the latest, triumphant episode in the old conflict between ordinary Americans, on the one side, and wealth and privilege, on the other side. This interpretation has considerable basis in fact, but it is far too simple an answer.

Other historians identified the core progressives more specifically as western and southern farmers who carried forward the long tradition of agrarian protest which went back at least to the eighteenth century and culminated in the Populist revolt of the 1890s. John D. Hicks first presented this interpretation in *The Populist Revolt* (1931). It was later restated and refined in C. Vann Woodward's *Origins of the New South, 1877–1913* (1951) and in Russel B. Nye's *Midwestern Progressive Politics* (1951). Hicks, Woodward, and Nye, like DeWitt, saw progressivism, fundamentally, as a popular crusade— a broadening of agrarian protest—to restore democracy and curtail the power of the large corporations, particularly the railroads and banks, which had oppressed the farmer. Like the first interpretation, the agrarian view of progressivism is not wrong, but it is too restricted.

In the early 1950s, historians began to answer the "who" question with a more critical appraisal of the political and socioeconomic forces which the progressives represented. This shift in view produced an urban, middle-class interpretation of progressivism which still dominates the literature on the subject. George E. Mowry and Alfred D. Chandler, Jr., assembled data on several hundred leading reformers and found them to be socially secure and well-educated men and women of Anglo-

Saxon Protestant stock who lived in cities and worked as businessmen, lawyers, and other professionals. Mowry first drew this profile in *The California Progressives* (1951); he later extended it to the entire nation in *The Era of Theodore Roosevelt* (1958). Chandler based his similar conclusions on a study of 260 leaders of the Progressive party of 1912 ("The Origins of Progressive Leadership," see below, p. 121). In Mowry's view, the old middle class felt caught or crushed between the growing power of large corporations and of labor unions. Leaders of the old middle class sought reforms to restore individualism and to restrain the forces of collectivism which they thought now dominated American society.

Building on the work of Mowry and Chandler, Richard Hofstadter gave the urban, middle-class interpretation of progressivism its fullest statement in *The Age of Reform: From Bryan to F.D.R.* (1955). This book, which was subtle and elegantly written and drew heavily upon the insights of sociology and psychology, answered the "who" question in a way that influenced a generation of historians. After the Civil War, Hofstadter said, members of the older middle classes, particularly ministers, lawyers, and college professors, who had long been acknowledged as the social and political leaders of their communities, found themselves increasingly overshadowed by a new governing elite of political bosses allied with railroads, corporations, and financiers. "It is my thesis," Hofstadter wrote, that men of the older middle class became progressives, "not because of economic deprivation but primarily because they were the victims of an upheaval in status that took place in the United States during the closing decades of the nineteenth and the early years of the twentieth century." Although Hofstadter was sympathetic to the progressives (indeed, he said that he wrote from "within" the reform tradition), he called attention to some of the dark characteristics of their movement which earlier historians had failed to note. Hofstadter's progressives were middle-class Protestants who undertook reform largely to solve their own personal problems. Self-righteous, moralistic, and culturally intolerant, they tended to settle for "ceremonial," rather than far-reaching, solutions. This increased their self-esteem but did not necessarily get at the root of problems.

After the publication of *The Age of Reform*, historians retained Hofstadter's critical stance but significantly reformulated the urban, middle-class interpretation. Samuel P. Hays (*The Response to Industrialism, 1885-1914*, 1957) and Robert H. Wiebe (*The Search for Order, 1877-1920*, 1967) were in the vanguard of this reformulation. In their view, the progressives were not the backward-looking men and women whom Mowry and Hofstadter had described; on the contrary, they were members of an assured, farsighted "new middle class" of physicians, businessmen, scientists, engineers, and social workers. They were determined to use their knowledge and skills to solve the problems caused by industrialization and to impose order upon a nearly chaotic society. To achieve their goals, the "new middle-class" reformers relied upon organization, the application of scientific (or social-scientific) expertise, and the value of efficiency and rationality. As Wiebe put it, "The heart of progressivism was the ambition of the new middle class to fulfill its destiny through bureaucratic means."

Some historians have argued that the most influential progressive reformers came from the wealthiest segments of American society. Wiebe's first book, *Businessmen and Reform: A Study of the Progressive Movement* (1962), depicted a divided business community, some of whose members played significant roles in the enactment of major economic reforms. The New-Left historian, Gabriel Kolko, made corporation leaders and financiers even more central to reform than Wiebe had done (*The Triumph of Conservatism: A Reinterpretation of American History, 1900-1916*, 1963). Kolko argued that the most powerful businessmen, especially those associated with the New York financial titan, J. Pierpont Morgan, were the main proponents—and the chief beneficiaries—of the regulatory measures adopted during the administrations of Presidents Theodore Roosevelt, William Howard Taft, and Woodrow Wilson.

Finally, J. Joseph Huthmacher and John D. Buenker have

called attention to the urban-immigrant sources of reform. Huthmacher first sketched the argument in "Urban Liberalism and the Age of Reform" (*Mississippi Valley Historical Review,* 1962), and Buenker fleshed it out eleven years later in *Urban Liberalism and Progressive Reform.* Unlike most historians discussed above, Huthmacher and Buenker did not insist that their group led progressivism, but they did make it clear that legislators who represented immigrant constituencies in the large cities of the East and Middle West gave critical support to reforms which benefited their people. These included measures for the regulation of business, for the promotion of social welfare, and for political reform to increase the influence of ordinary voters.

Each of the historians just discussed has made an important contribution to our understanding of progressivism. But most of them have tended to claim that their key progressives placed a distinctive stamp on the entire movement; they have also tended to define progressivism in such a way as to substantiate that claim. Obviously, these historians cannot all be right.

No interpretation has been more sharply criticized than Hofstadter's status-revolution theory. Almost as soon as he presented it, critics correctly pointed out that he had neglected to compare the progressives with a control group of conservatives in order to determine whether his reformers were significantly different from their opponents. It was not long before a number of scholars had produced evidence which revealed that both progressive and conservative political leaders fitted the Mowry-Chandler-Hofstadter profile: educated, well-off businessmen, lawyers, and professionals. As David P. Thelen put it in a searching and influential study of the Wisconsin legislature: "The 'typical' progressive and conservative came from the same social background" ("Social Tensions and the Origins of Progressivism," *Journal of American History,* 1969).

The chief deficiency of the "status-revolution" and other "middle-class" interpretations of progressivism is the virtual meaninglessness of the term "middle class" with reference to the United States at the turn of the century. Of course most businessmen, lawyers, doctors, ministers, and other professionals enjoyed middle-class status. But so also did skilled workers, merchants, farmers who were not tenants or sharecroppers, and myriad others. Indeed, except for the very rich and the very poor, most Americans were in the middle classes. Neither Hofstadter nor his critics and successors have done anything to help us to get out of the dilemma created by the loose and vague use of the adjective "middle class."

Works by Hays and Wiebe have stood the test of time better than *The Age of Reform*. Their interpretations placed progressivism in the context of what Wiebe has called "the process of America's modernization" and described the contributions to reform of businessmen and professionals ("The Progressive Years, 1900–1917," see below, p. 120). Yet in focusing so sharply on important economic changes and broad social groupings, Hays and Wiebe passed over some of the most important aspects of progressive reform—the great popularity of individual leaders, the widespread anger at the corruption which they exposed, and the exhilaration of reformers when they defeated a hated boss or businessman. Hays' and Wiebe's expert progressives seem too faceless and too bland and passionless ever to have led the frenetic battles for reform that broke out all across the United States in the early 1900s. Their interpretations err even more significantly in underrating the major roles in progressivism which farmers, workers, and immigrants played.

The advocates of the middle-class view might reply that they intended to study the leaders of reform, not its supporters, to identify and describe the men and women who imparted the dominant character to progressivism, not its mass base. The study of leadership is surely a valid subject in its own right and is particularly useful for an understanding of progressivism. But too much focus on leadership conceals more than it discloses about early twentieth-century reform. The dynamics of progressivism were crucially generated by ordinary people—by the sometimes frenzied mass supporters of progressive leaders, by rank-and-file voters willing to trust a reform candidate. The chronology of progressivism can be traced by events which aroused large numbers of people—a sensational muckraking article, an outrageous political scandal, an eye-opening legislative investigation, or a tragic social calamity. Events such as these gave reform its rhythm and its power.

Progressivism cannot be understood without seeing how the masses of Americans perceived and responded to such events. Widely circulated magazines gave people everywhere the sordid facts of corruption and carried the clamor for reform into every city, village, and county. State and national election campaigns enabled progressive candidates to trumpet their programs. Almost no literate person in the United States in, say, 1906 could have been unaware that ten-year-old children worked through the night in dangerous factories, or that many United States senators served big business. Progressivism was the only reform movement ever experienced by the whole American nation. Its national appeal and mass base vastly exceeded that of Jacksonian reform. And progressivism's dependence on the people for its objectives and timing has no comparison in the executive-dominated New Deal of Franklin D. Roosevelt or the Great Society of Lyndon B. Johnson. Wars and depressions had previously engaged the whole nation, but never reform. And so we are back to the problem of how to explain and define the outpouring of progressive reform which excited and involved so many different kinds of people.

A little more than a decade ago, Buenker and Thelen recognized the immense diversity of progressivism and suggested ways in which to reorient the study of early twentieth-century reform. Buenker observed that divergent groups often came together on one issue and then changed alliances on the next ("The Progressive Era: A Search for a Synthesis," *Mid-America,* 1969). Indeed, different reformers sometimes favored the same measure for distinctive, even opposite, reasons. Progressivism could be understood only in the light of these shifting coalitions. Thelen, in his study of Wisconsin's legislature, also emphasized the importance of cooperation between different reform groups. "The basic riddle in Progressivism," he concluded, "is not what drove groups apart but what made them seek common cause."

There is a great deal of wisdom in these articles, particularly in their recognition of the diversity of progressivism and in the concept of shifting coalitions of reformers. A two-pronged approach is necessary to carry forward this way of looking at early twentieth-century reform. First, we should study, not an imaginary unified progressive movement, but individual reforms and give particular attention to the goals of their diverse supporters, the public rationales given for them, and the results which they achieved. Second, we should try to identify the features which were more or less common to different progressive reforms.

The first task—distinguishing the goals of a reform from its rhetoric and its results—is more difficult than it might appear to be. Older interpretations of progressivism implicitly assumed that the rhetoric explained the goals and that, if a proposed reform became law, the results fulfilled the intentions behind it. Neither assumption is a sound one: purposes, rationale, and results are three different things. Samuel P. Hays' influential article, "The Politics of Reform in Municipal Government in the Progressive Era" *(Pacific Northwest Quarterly,* 1964), exposed the fallacy of automatically equating the democratic rhetoric of the reformers with their true purposes. The two may have coincided, but the historian has to demonstrate that fact, not take it for granted. The unexamined identification of either intentions or rhetoric with results is also invalid, although it is still a common feature of the scholarship on progressivism. Only within the last decade have historians begun to examine the actual achievements of the reformers. To carry out this first task, in the following chapters we will distinguish between the goals and rhetoric of individual reforms and will discuss the results of reform whenever the current literature permits. To do so is to observe the ironies, complexities, and disappointments of progressivism.

The second task—that of identifying the common characteristics of progressivism—is even more difficult than the first but is an essential base on which to build an understanding of progressivism. The rest of this chapter focuses on identifying such characteristics. The place to begin that effort is the origins of progressivism.

THE ORIGINS OF PROGRESSIVISM

The profound economic and social changes of the last third of the nineteenth century created the conditions to which the progressive reformers responded. The most striking transformation—and the one which energized many others—was the rise of new gigantic corporations which absorbed their competitors and integrated every process of production and marketing. Steel and oil were but the two most dramatic examples of industries in which the scale and extent of operations dwarfed anything ever seen before. The largest corporations, popularly called "trusts," frightened people because they were not only rich and powerful but, worse still, seemed to threaten what Americans cherished dearly—the equality of economic opportunity, or the right of everyone to get ahead. Moreover, the fate of each person was now to a large degree determined by distant forces which he or she neither saw, understood, nor controlled. The cost of railway services in Kansas, the price of beef in Georgia, and wages paid in California all depended in significant part upon decisions made in such faraway places as London, New York, or Chicago.

Farmers and workers experienced directly the effects of these decisions. Growers of wheat, corn, cotton, and tobacco —the great staples of American agriculture—found themselves the victims, not only of banks and railroads, but also of an international market system. The prices which farmers received for their products declined steadily after the Civil War; at the same time, many heretofore independent rural families became tenants. Workers now labored in huge mines, factories, and plants which were both dangerous and strange. They were strange because of the unnatural rhythms of work governed by the factory clock, the routine and unfulfilling work, and the diversity of languages and religions of fellow workers. They were dangerous because the machines killed or maimed hundreds of thousands of workers each year. Wages rose during good times, but the times were often bad, and the violence of strikes reddened the landscape. By the 1890s, industrial strife had become so common a feature of life in the United States that many persons believed that their society was falling apart.

Nowhere were the passions and problems greater than in the large cities, where crowded people competed with each other for jobs and a decent place to live and clashed over beliefs and ways of living. Great numbers of city people had come from the American countryside in search of a better standard of living; other millions had come for the same reason from Italy, Austria-Hungary, and Russia. Most of the immigrants from Europe were Jewish or Roman Catholic, and their cultures and lifestyles, even their presence, came under attack by native-born Americans, especially during hard times. Even during prosperous times, the density of urban population strained the facilities upon which decent life depended. Municipal governments were expected to provide pure water, adequate transportation, and good schools, but they commonly lacked the administrative ability to do so. Political parties frequently integrated the widely separated agencies of urban government and met the needs of the lower classes. But middle- and upper-class urbanites usually regarded this as a corrupt system, not as a means of enabling the poor to survive.

Americans of the 1870s and 1880s resented and resisted the hardships which they had to endure. Their reactions anticipated and inspired progressivism, but they differed from it in many respects. Hays and Wiebe have correctly observed that many of the responses and reforms of this earlier era were relatively simple solutions, or panaceas, which attempted to restore traditional ways and to remedy the worst consequences of industrialization with a single stroke. Thelen has shown how reformers of the 1880s were isolated from each other; seemingly unaware of their common problems, the various reform groups went their own way in advocating solutions (*The New Citizenship: Origins of Progressivism in Wisconsin, 1885–1900*, 1972). Not until the 1890s would a coherent intellectual critique of existing conditions emerge; not until after 1900 would diverse dissatisfied Americans come together in support of progressive reforms. Until then, they carried on separate, and largely unsuccessful, campaigns for change.

Businessmen of the age were by no means fully able to dominate the economic forces set in motion by the wealthiest members of their group. Price wars, depressions, and the uncertain access to human and material resources constantly frustrated them. Owners of the largest corporations faced the baffling difficulties of profitably running far-flung operations; during hard times, they were grateful just to cover the rising fixed costs of their huge enterprises. Confronted by chaotic conditions, businessmen experimented with a succession of devices to substitute cooperation for competition: *pools* (or cartels) which fixed prices and divided up the market; *trusts* which consolidated several companies under the central authority of a single board; and *holding companies*, a legal creation which permitted the joint direction of previously independent enterprises. None of these inventions satisfied most businessmen; each, moreover, heightened the outrage which other people felt toward the large corporations.

Western and southern farmers of the 1870s and 1880s also looked to their own organizations to alleviate their problems. The most important of these organizations were the Grange, which flourished in the late 1860s and early 1870s, and the National Farmers' Alliance, which spread eastward and northward from Texas and reached the peak of its strength about 1890. Under Grange pressure, many midwestern and southern states adopted legislation for the control of railroad rates and services; however, most of these efforts fell victims of judicial annulment or administrative palsy. Both the Grange and the Alliance established cooperatives to buy and sell, but they usually failed on account of mismanagement and the counterattack of merchants and brokers. From 1877 to 1884, farmers joined with workers in a third party, the Greenback Labor party, but, again, with no long-lasting results.

Workers, too, resisted the consequences of industrialization. Whether from the countryside of Illinois or of Poland, many of them found the factory intolerable and refused to conform to its discipline and culture. One solution was to go back to the homeland, which many of the immigrants did. The Knights of Labor, a secret society organized in local chapters without regard to skill or trade, flourished in the mid-1880s after some successful strikes. But the Knights of Labor could not (and did not) survive for long because its leaders refused to recognize that the wage system was permanent, opposed strikes, and sought the return of an imagined classless society in which each worker was also an entrepreneur. Sensing that such ideas were obsolete, skilled workers joined trade unions associated with the new American Federation of Labor because it frankly welcomed industrialization and accepted the wage system.

Other groups came forward with their own panaceas. During the 1880s, in the eastern and midwestern cities, well-educated men of secure social status, called Mugwumps, became deeply alarmed by the alleged corruption of party politics and their own exclusion from power. They were Republicans for the most part, yet they bolted the GOP to protest against James G. Blaine, the party's allegedly sordid candidate in the presidential election of 1884. Many of them abandoned their party in local and state contests as well. The Mugwumps' chief remedy for political corruption was the civil-service system, that is, the making of appointments to public office on the basis of merit, rather than service to a political party. Politicians mocked the Mugwumps and sneered at the "snivel service," but the reformers succeeded in getting the civil-service principle written into national law in 1883, following the assassination two years earlier of President James A. Garfield by a disappointed office seeker.

In the economic sphere, too, there was no dearth of panaceas for the nation's problems. Henry George's eloquent *Progress and Poverty* (1879) argued that a single tax on land would return the unearned increment in land values to society and restore complete equality of opportunity. Another popular remedy was antitrust legislation. More than twenty states adopted antitrust statutes during the 1880s; the federal government followed suit in 1890, as did other states afterward. The free and unlimited coinage of silver at a ratio of sixteen-to-one to gold (which greatly overpriced silver relative to its market value) was another panacea. Many persons thought that it would miraculously increase the prices of agricultural products and redistribute wealth. Social problems, too, inspired surefire solutions, particularly the prohibition of the manufacture and sale of alcoholic beverages.

It is not surprising that reformers of the late nineteenth century had little to do with one another. Their protests and programs had in common neither cause nor objective; each addressed a single problem. Few reform movements were based upon an understanding of the fundamental economic and social processes of this time. But we are able to make this judgment only with the benefit of long hindsight. Reformers of the 1870s and 1880s were suddenly engulfed in a maelstrom of change which they could not possibly have fully understood. For example, there is no reason why discontented Americans should have foreseen that large-scale, bureaucratic industrialism was to be permanent and therefore should have made their peace with it. The reform campaigns of the 1870s and 1880s were largely unsuccessful; even so, they contributed significant methods and ideas to early twentieth-century reform. Railroad regulation, trust-busting, temperance, and almost every other remedy of the late 1800s would come up again after 1900 and be more ferociously fought over than ever. They would also be part of a generalized impulse toward reform. Before this coalescence of reform movements could occur, however, a national crisis first had to discredit the reigning social and political ideas of the day.

Many respectable Americans in the last third of the nineteenth century scorned protest and reform and articulated a conservative defense of the status quo. The conservative doctrines were presented as timeless truths confirmed by science; and, together, they formed what Eric F. Goldman has called the "steel chain of ideas" (*Rendezvous with Destiny: A History of Modern American Reform,* 1952). The chain's great strength lay in the assertion that what existed was right and good—or, at least, inevitable—and could not be changed without great damage to the human race. This belief, so-called social Darwinism, was derived by the English sociologist, Herbert Spencer, from the biological evolutionary theory of Charles Darwin (*Origin of Species*, 1859). Social Darwinism provided a seemingly scientific rationale with which to oppose governmental interference in social and economic affairs. Spencer visited the United States in 1882 and was lavishly feted by the intellectual and business elite. But Spencer actually won few disciples in the United States because his harsh doctrines were unacceptable to the vast majority of Americans (for example, he opposed public schools and said that governments should let poor people starve rather than feed them).

More deeply embedded in American traditions than social Darwinism were three other conservative doctrines: the defense of weak government, the denial of class conflict, and loyalty to the two major political parties. All were conservative barricades against progressivism.

Conservative Americans of the business and commercial classes came relatively late and somewhat disingenuously to the doctrine of weak government. During the first half of the nineteenth century, the slogan "That government is best which governs least" had been the battle cry of Jeffersonians and Jacksonians to protest against the control of government by the upper class to advance its own interests. Only in the latter part of the nineteenth century, when state governments began to adopt laws to protect workers, advance social welfare, and—as businessmen claimed—to threaten prosperity, did conservatives discover the virtues of laissez faire and, for a time, impart their doctrines to the courts. Even then, businessmen kept up their traditional demands for governmental policies to stimulate industrial growth and commercial enterprise. Conservatives lauded weak government and quoted Herbert Spencer when it served their interest to do so, but such rhetoric testified more to their doctrinal flexibility than to their sincerity. The belief in weak government, or the pretense of such belief, was only a wooden barricade against progressivism.

The denial of any conflict of interests among the classes proved to be a stronger conservative barricade. Americans of every class were shocked by the violent industrial and labor strife of the late nineteenth century and tried to convince themselves that such social disharmony would not last. Conservatives played on that conviction and used it in their arguments against such policies as special protection for workers. Americans who had benefited from governmental privileges had always insisted that the producing interests of the nation were fundamentally harmonious, and that what benefited one group helped everyone. So deeply ingrained was the doctrine of the harmony of economic interests in common-sense philosophy and American traditions, that progressives could only scorch, not burn to the ground, the conservatives' barricade of the denial of class conflict. Indeed, progressives could never come to one mind about the inevitability of class and group differences.

Firm allegiance to the major political parties was a third barrier against reform. To be sure, business leaders did not always find Republican and Democratic politicians to be reliable. Machine-run governments in the large cities did often tax the rich in order the help the poor. But the state and national parties were safer; to conservatives, they were shields against third parties of inflationists, workers, and farmers. Nationwide and heterogeneous, the Democratic and Republican parties gratified supporters of the status quo by massive inaction when it came to "class legislation" assisting special groups in the population. Yet despite their reluctance to endorse new policies, the major parties still could count on the support of the majority of adult males on election day. Conservatives, when they extolled the virtue of loyalty to a major party, were simply reinforcing the beliefs of most men. It would require a major depression and an accompanying political crisis during the 1890s to weaken this and the other conservative doctrinal barricades. When the crises were over, progressivism had already begun to take definite shape.

The 1890s began with a severe decline in agricultural prices which propelled angry southern and western farmers into the most radical phase of the agrarian revolt. For several years prior to 1890, lecturers for the Farmers' Alliance had been touring the South and the Plains states. They explained to farmers the alleged causes of their misery and exhorted them to get together and take control of their own destinies. The sharp decline in agricultural prices inflamed the camp-meeting fervor engendered by the Alliance lecturers. This in turn created a mass base for the new Populist party launched at Omaha, Nebraska, in 1892. The Populist platform of that year shrewdly combined a radical critique of existing political and economic conditions with a series of proposals specifically designed to benefit farmers, such as the national ownership of railroads, a plan to support crop prices and provide abundant credit to farmers, a graduated income tax, and so on. Democratic and Republican campaigners denounced the Populists as dangerous lunatics, but the Populists won nearly 9 per cent of the total vote for President in 1892 and elected numerous state and local candidates.

Less than a year later, economic depression struck the nation. Some three to four million persons were unemployed during the winter of 1893–1894, and tens of thousands of "tramps" searched the countryside for food. The Democratic President, Grover Cleveland, sat by in the firm conviction that it was no part of the government's job to relieve either urban or rural distress. More than that, Cleveland made it clear that he would not tolerate protest. When a strike against the Pullman Palace Car Company spread to the railroads in Chicago in the summer of 1894, Cleveland sent in federal troops who used their guns to subdue the strikers. That same year, Jacob Coxey's tattered little army, which had marched from Ohio to Washington to demand a federal program of public works, was clubbed down as it approached the Capitol.

The depression and such outbreaks of violence caused

many Americans to ponder the apparent failure of their institutions. Were political democracy and equality of economic opportunity possible in an urban-industrial society? More searching answers were now given to that question than ever before in American history. Some of them came from a new generation of ministers, social workers, and settlement-house workers who lived with and worked among poor people in the cities. Walter Rauschenbusch, who later became the prophet of the Social Gospel, was a young minister of a Baptist mission in New York during the depression. He could never forget the endless throngs of men out of work, food, clothing, and shelter during the winter of 1893–1894. "They wore down our threshold," he later wrote, "and they wore away our hearts. . . . One could hear human virtue cracking and crumbling all around." Other responses to the depression came from the authors of a new literature of exposure which would soon flower into muck-raking journalism. The most popular of these early exposés was Henry Demarest Lloyd's *Wealth Against Commonwealth* (1894), a scathing indictment of the Standard Oil Company. Victims of the depression, as well as those persons who experienced its miseries through the writings of others, were not likely to believe again that active government was immoral, that class conflict existed only in the minds of a few agitators, and that the existing major parties could solve the nation's problems.

The most immediate consequence of the crises of the mid-1890s was a series of movements for urban reform. Although they varied from city to city, these campaigns were all able to win united support from diverse elements. In many eastern cities, reform was led by businessmen and professionals who said that efficiency and economy were essential during a time of depression and that the existing political parties could not provide them. Many of these reformers were former Mug-wumps, but now they were not oblivious to the problems of poor people. On the contrary, these reformers often won the support of voters in the tenement districts by paying attention to their needs. Perhaps above all, the "good-government" reformers, as they were called, expressed the antagonism toward the party bosses and machines which persons in almost every social group were beginning to feel by the mid-1890s. An even more democratic type of urban reform appeared in the Middle West, where arrogant utility and street-car companies, rather than corrupt party machines, were the main targets of the reformers. By emphasizing depression-related issues, such as rate reduction, economy, and the equalization of the tax burden, these midwestern dissidents succeeded even better than the eastern "good-government" reformers in uniting formerly antagonistic groups.

The various crises of the 1890s culminated in 1896 in a realigning election which shattered the Populist party and insured the dominance of the GOP in national politics until 1932. In brief, the Democrats absorbed the Populist party but in doing so had to retain a measure of the rhetoric of agrarian protest. The Democrats also demanded the unlimited coinage of silver at the ratio of sixteen-to-one; this drove many industrial workers, who feared higher prices for food, into the Republican fold. Thus the Republicans succeeded in labeling the Democrats as dangerous radicals and enemies of sound money and low prices. The chief actors in the drama of 1896 were the Democrat, William Jennings Bryan of Nebraska, who was no radical but who did demand free silver, and the Republican, William McKinley of Ohio, who gave the appearance of being able to reduce social tensions by bringing back prosperity.

Prosperity did return after McKinley's election, but the pain and suffering of the 1890s were not forgotten. Nor was the conviction that it was urgently necessary to reshape political institutions so that they could cope with the still pressing problems of an urban-industrial society. Just beginning to join forces for this task were men and women who would call themselves progressives. Not for almost another decade after McKinley's election did their diverse reform movements come fully into their own, but many of progressivism's features could be seen fairly clearly by about 1900.

THE CHARACTER AND SPIRIT OF PROGRESSIVISM

Progressivism was characterized, in the first place, by a distinctive set of attitudes toward industrialism. By the turn of the century, the overwhelming majority of Americans had accepted the permanence of large-scale industrial, commercial, and financial enterprises and of the wage and factory systems. The progressives shared this attitude. Most were not socialists, and they undertook reform, not to dismantle modern economic institutions, but rather to ameliorate and improve the conditions of industrial life. Yet progressivism was infused with a deep outrage against the worst consequences of industrialism. Outpourings of anger at corporate wrongdoing and of hatred for industry's callous pursuit of profit frequently punctuated the course of reform in the early twentieth century. Indeed, anti-business emotion was a prime mover of progressivism. That the acceptance of industrialism *and* the outrage against it were intrinsic to early twentieth-century reform does not mean that progressivism was mindless or that it has to be considered indefinable. But it does suggest that there was a powerful irony in progressivism: reforms which gained support from a people angry with the oppressive aspects of industrialism also assisted the same persons to accommodate to it, albeit to an industrialism which was to some degree socially responsible.

The progressives' ameliorative reforms also reflected their faith in progress—in mankind's ability, through purposeful action, to improve the environment and the conditions of life. The late nineteenth-century dissidents had not lacked this faith, but their espousal of panaceas bespoke a deep pessimism: "Unless this one great change is made, things will get worse." Progressive reforms were grounded on a broader assumption. In particular, reforms could protect the people hurt by industrialization and make the environment more humane. For intellectuals of the era, the achievement of such goals meant that they had to meet Herbert Spencer head on and confute his absolute "truths." Progressive thinkers, led by Lester Frank

Ward, Richard T. Ely, and, most important, John Dewey, demolished social Darwinism with what Goldman has called "reform Darwinism." They asserted that human adaptation to the environment did not interfere with the evolutionary process, but was, rather, part and parcel of the law of natural change. Progressive intellectuals and their popularizers produced a vast literature to condemn laissez faire and to promote the concept of the active state.

To improve the environment meant, above all, to intervene in economic and social affairs in order to control natural forces and impose a measure of order upon them. This belief in interventionism was a third component of progressivism. It was visible in almost every reform of the era, from the supervision of business to the prohibition of alcohol (John W. Chambers II, *The Tyranny of Change: America in the Progressive Era, 1900–1917*, 1980). Interventionism could be both private and public. Given their choice, most progressives preferred to work noncoercively through voluntary organizations for economic and social changes. However, as time passed, it became evident that most progressive reforms could be achieved only by legislation and public control. Such an extension of public authority made many progressives uneasy, and few of them went so far as Herbert Croly in glorifying the state in his *The Promise of American Life* (1909) and *Progressive Democracy* (1914). Even so, the intervention necessary for their reforms inevitably propelled progressives toward an advocacy of the use of governmental power. A familiar scenario during the period was one in which progressives called upon public authorities to assume responsibility for interventions which voluntary organizations had begun.

The foregoing describes the basic characteristics of progressivism but says little about its ideals. Progressivism was inspired by two bodies of belief and knowledge—evangelical Protestantism and the natural and social sciences. These sources of reform may appear at first glance antagonistic to one another. Actually, they were complementary, and each imparted distinctive qualities to progressivism.

Ever since the religious revivals from about 1820 to 1840, evangelical Protestantism had spurred reform in the United States. Basic to the reform mentality was an all-consuming urge to purge the world of sin, such as the sins of slavery and intemperance, against which nineteenth-century reformers had crusaded. Now the progressives carried the struggle into the modern citadels of sin—the teeming cities of the nation. No one can read their writings and speeches without being struck by the fact that many of them believed that it was their Christian duty to right the wrongs created by the processes of industrialization. Such belief was the motive force behind the Social Gospel, a movement which swept through the Prostestant churches in the 1890s and 1900s. Its goal was to align churches, frankly and aggressively, on the side of the downtrodden, the poor, and working people—in other words, to make Christianity relevant to this world, not the next. It is difficult to measure the influence of the Social Gospel, but it seared the consciences of millions of Americans, particularly in urban areas. And it triumphed in the organization in 1908 of the Federal Council of Churches of Christ in America, with its platform which condemned exploitative capitalism and proclaimed the right of workers to organize and to enjoy a decent standard of living. Observers at the Progressive party's national convention of 1912 should not have been surprised to hear the delegates sing, spontaneously and emotionally, the Christian call to arms, "Onward, Christian Soldiers!"

The faith which inspired the singing of "Onward, Christian Soldiers!" had significant implications for progressive reforms. Progressives used moralistic appeals to make people feel the awful weight of wrong in the world and to exhort them to accept personal responsibility for its eradication. The resultant reforms could be generous in spirit, but they could also seem intolerant to the people who were "reformed." Progressivism sometimes seemed to envision life in a small-town Protestant community or an urban drawing room—a vision sharply different from that of Catholic or Jewish immigrants. Not every progressive shared the evangelical ethos, much less its intolerance, but few of the era's reforms were untouched by the spirit and techniques of Protestant revivalism.

Science also had a pervasive impact on the methods and objectives of progressivism. Many leading reformers were specialists in the new disciplines of statistics, economics, sociology, and psychology. These new social scientists set out to gather data on human behavior as it actually was and to discover the laws which governed it. Since social scientists accepted environmentalist and interventionist assumptions implicitly, they believed that knowledge of natural laws would make it possible to devise and apply solutions to improve the human condition. This faith underpinned the optimism of most progressives and predetermined the methods used by almost all reformers of the time: investigation of the facts and application of social-science knowledge to their analysis; entrusting trained experts to decide what should be done; and, finally, mandating government to execute reform.

These methods may have been rational, but they were also compatible with progressive moralism. In its formative period, American social science was heavily infused with ethical concerns. An essential purpose of statistics, economics, sociology, and psychology was to improve and uplift. Leading practitioners of these disciplines, for example, Richard T. Ely, an economist at the University of Wisconsin, were often in the vanguard of the Social Gospel. Progressives blended science and religion into a view of human behavior which was unique to their generation, which had grown up in an age of revivals and come to maturity at the birth of social science.

All of progressivism's distinctive features found expression in muckraking—the literary spearhead of early twentieth-century reform. Through the medium of such new ten-cent magazines as *McClure's*, *Everybody's*, and *Cosmopolitan*, the muckrakers exposed every dark aspect and corner of American life. Nothing escaped the probe of writers such as Ida M. Tarbell, Lincoln Steffens, Ray Stannard Baker, and Burton J. Hendrick—not big business, politics, prostitution, race relations, or even the churches. Behind the exposés of the muckrakers lay the progressive attitude toward industrialism: it was here to stay, but many of its aspects seemed to be deplorable. These could be improved, however, if only people became aware of conditions and determined to ameliorate them. To bring about such awareness, the muckrakers appealed to their readers' consciences. Steffens' famous series, published in book form as *The Shame of the Cities* in 1904, was frankly intended to make people feel guilty for the corruption which riddled their cities. The muckrakers also used the social scientists' method of the careful and painstaking gathering of data—and with devastating effects. This investigative function—which was later largely taken over by governmental agencies—proved absolutely vital to educating and arousing Americans.

All progressive crusades shared the spirit and used the techniques discussed here, but they did so to different degrees and in different ways. Some voiced a greater willingness to accept industrialism and even to extol its potential benefits; others expressed more strongly the outrage against its darker aspects. Some intervened through voluntary organizations; others relied on government to achieve changes. Each reform reflected a distinctive balance between the claims of Protestant moralism and of scientific rationalism. Progressives fought among themselves over these questions even while they set to the common task of applying their new methods and ideas to the problems of a modern society.

TWO

A Transformation
of Politics
and Government

Despite the economic crises and electoral realignment of the
1890s, politics in the United States had not changed much by
the time an assassin's bullet made Theodore Roosevelt President
of the United States in September 1901. In fact, some developments in the late 1890s actually obscured the challenges
posed by economic and social changes to the usual forms of
politics and government. The quick and smashing victory in the

war with Spain in 1898 boosted national pride and self-confidence. Prosperity returned quickly during McKinley's administration. Particularly important, the dominant Republican party seemed to stand for policies which would promote economic growth and harmony. And Roosevelt had taken office with the pledge to "continue, absolutely unbroken, the policy of President McKinley."

Yet the upheavals of the 1890s, particularly the labor violence and class conflicts of that decade, had left an enduring mark. Many Americans believed that government ought to act forcefully to diminish group differences, but few of them knew what government *could* do. A wave of industrial and railroad consolidations from 1897 to 1904 focused new attention on the problem of the "trusts." During the same period, organized labor experienced unprecedented growth: the membership of the AFL surged from 256,000 in 1897 to 1,676,000 in 1904. It was, altogether, a spectacular and sudden consolidation of economic power, and it worried many ordinary people.

Men and women in other sectors of the society also banded together in special-interest groups. Some were drawn to one another by common economic interests, some by shared professional and cultural interests; still others were committed to "reform" in general. Whatever held them together, these groups moved into politics with a vengeance. The fact that it was difficult for the major parties to satisfy special-interest groups simply energized the group members further.

These developments had implications of great significance for the traditional patterns of political participation and governance. Since the Jacksonian era, voting for a *party* had been the chief means of political expression by the masses of people, and allegiance to a party had been one of the most important forms of personal identification. Election campaigns were exciting affairs, with numerous allurements such as torchlight parades, picnics, and mass meetings. Most adult males chose their parties on the basis of long-standing sectional, cultural, and communal influences and passed their loyalties on to their sons. The memory of the Civil War was a strong stimulus to partisanship, as were ethnic and religious conflicts. It was rare indeed when individuals or groups could find a way to influence governmental policies other than through the instrumentality of a party.

The fact that they enjoyed access to the formulation of public policy only very indirectly through parties probably did not worry many Americans in the late nineteenth century. Public policies, in fact, had a limited impact upon them. Government remained almost as weak as it had been before the Civil War. At every level, the legislature was the dominant branch, and its members were largely concerned with the needs of their local constituencies. The characteristic public policy was the extension of privileges and the distribution of resources to enterprising individuals and corporations. Regulation was recognized as a function of government, especially in the states, but effective administrative structures to carry out such regulation were virtually nonexistent.

Yet by the opening of the new century there was a growing perception that the old political and governmental structures were incapable of meeting the needs of a new urban-industrial society. However, the path to political change was strewn with obstacles. One was the historic American devotion to weak government and local autonomy. Another was the long-standing abhorrence of what was called "class legislation" which recognized the different needs of clashing groups. But the most important barrier to change was party loyalty. That loyalty had been weakened by the turmoil of the 1890s, but the emotional and historic bonds of party allegiance were still very strong in 1900. Each of these obstacles to political and governmental change would come under assault during the progressive era.

PROGRESSIVISM
IN THE CITIES AND STATES

Political progressivism originated in the cities. Although state and national governance might well remain remote and even irrelevant to many persons, tolerable life (at times, literal survival) in crowded urban areas required sanitation, police protection, and social services. For example, Pittsburgh, because of its impure water supply, had one of the highest rates of death from typhoid fever, dysentery, and cholera of any large city in the world. Political party machines seemed to many people to be too corrupt to provide the services which an urban population required, while traditional governmental structures remained too rudimentary to meet their needs.

There were two general kinds of movements for the reform and modernization of city governments. One was led by businessmen and professionals who resented the corruption and inefficiency of the party machines. This resentment, triggered by disclosures of fraud and by the breakdown of city services during the depression of the 1890s, had set off a wave of municipal reform campaigns on behalf of nonpartisan candidates who promised "honest, efficient, and businesslike" government. The merchant William L. Strong, Mayor of New York City from 1895 to 1897, typified this kind of reformer. The other type of municipal progressivism grew out of the urban masses' pressing need for city services and economic relief and was typified in the career of Hazen S. Pingree, Mayor of Detroit from 1890 to 1897. Compared to Strong, Pingree gave more attention to welfare services, regulation of utility and trolley companies, and the redistribution of Detroit's tax burden. By 1900, various combinations of the Strong and Pingree approaches were being tried all across the country. Urban progressivism was on the threshold of its most creative phase.

Much of this creative thought and energy went toward eliminating what James Bryce, the great English observer of American politics at this time, called the "mechanical defects in the structure of municipal government." Many reformers believed that the salvation of the cities lay in greatly enlarging the powers of the mayor, heretofore usually a figurehead; electing councilmen from the city at large, instead of by wards; reducing state interference in city affairs; and by making administrative appointments only according to civil-service rules. In 1899, the National Municipal League, organized in 1894, incorporated these and other reforms in its model city charter. An even more drastic remedy for "mechanical defects" originated in Galveston, Texas, in 1901. After a hurricane devastated that city, the mayor and council were replaced by a nonpartisan administrative commission. Des Moines, Iowa, adopted a version of the commission plan in 1908, as did hundreds of medium-sized cities during the next decade. A further refinement of the commission plan, government by a city manager responsible to an elected council, also gained widespread acceptance after 1913. Melvin G. Holli (*Reform in Detroit: Hazen S. Pingree and Urban Politics,* 1969) has called these manifestations of municipal progressivism "structural reform."

Another kind of municipal progressivism—what Holli has called "social reform"—swept through the larger cities after 1900. Pingree was the pioneer in this movement, but the most influential innovator was Tom L. Johnson, Mayor of Cleveland from 1901 to 1909. A wealthy businessman who was a convert to municipal socialism, Johnson forced Cleveland's utilities, railroads, and trolley companies to pay more taxes, and he won his fight for lower trolley fares. In Jersey City, Mark M. Fagan, an obscure undertaker, became mayor in 1901 and put together a comprehensive program designed, as he put it, "to make Jersey City a pleasant place to live in." This meant better schools, sewers, hospitals, playgrounds, and public concerts; it meant, as well, increasing the tax burden on the railroads and public-utility corporations. Through such programs as these, Johnson, Fagan, and other municipal progressives of their type did much to humanize their cities.

Actually the distinction between urban "structural reform" and "social reform" was often less sharp than Holli has made it. Martin J. Schiesl has demonstrated that there was no real contradiction between the two types of reform, and that in many cities structural and social reforms went hand in hand and reinforced each other (*The Politics of Efficiency: Municipal*

Administration and Reform in America, 1880–1920, 1977). Structural changes encouraged the popular belief that a city, now that it operated on a "businesslike" basis, could safely undertake new services, while social reforms promoted demands for structural changes to increase efficiency.

While the cities were experiencing reform at the beginning of the 1900s, much less was happening in the states and the nation. In the Middle West, an intense factionalism within the Republican party was just beginning to take on ideological overtones. Governor Robert M. La Follette of Wisconsin (1901–1906), the passionate leader of his state's dissidents, mobilized angry farmers, ethnics, and workers into a powerful coalition which won the direct primary, the regulation of railroads, the increased taxation of corporations, and the progressive income tax. Albert B. Cummins used similar issues against the entrenched Republican state machine to win the governorship of Iowa in 1901. La Follette and Cummins were not alone, but they and their counterparts were still widely scattered and isolated in 1904. In Washington, Roosevelt was beginning to take some initiatives, but his main concern before 1905 was his own reelection. Despite the apparent quietude, a political storm was about to engulf the country.

The storm burst in 1905 and intensified in 1906. While the muckrakers trumpeted the details, a number of states and cities witnessed shocking discoveries of the extent to which businessmen bribed legislators, conspired with party chieftains, and bought nominations. A legislative investigation of life-insurance companies in New York State in 1905 unexpectedly revealed the details of a long-standing alliance between Republican politicians and executives of the life-insurance companies. The companies received legislative protection, and the politicians received bribes and campaign funds in return. Graft trials of city officials in Pittsburgh and San Francisco in 1905 and 1906 uncovered a network of corruption of almost unbelievable proportions. Politics in South Dakota also exploded over the issue of business-political corruption, and insurgent Republicans captured the state in 1906 by capitalizing on the issue of railroad influence in politics. Democratic reform candidates won governorships in Alabama, Georgia, and Mississippi on the issue of business and railroad control of state houses. And so it went all across the nation. Party platforms everywhere in 1906 rang out against business control of politics; in the following winter, most governors, in their annual messages, joined in the demand for remedial legislation.

The response was immediate and overwhelming, and what had hitherto been scattered and isolated movements for state reform became a nationwide crusade. Legislatures regulated lobbying, forbade campaign contributions by corporations, and, in the unkindest cut of all, forbade railroads to issue free passes to legislators and other state officials. Almost all states instituted the direct primary for nominations in order to take control of them from bosses bribed by railroads and corporations. Perhaps of chief importance, most states greatly expanded their regulation of railroads, utilities, and other corporations and established administrative instrumentalities (usually independent "scientific" commissions) to make certain that regulation would be effective. From 1905 to 1907 alone, fifteen new state railroad commissions were established, and the powers of at least as many existing boards were expanded. Most of these commissions now had the power to set rates and to supervise service, safety, and financial operations. Within a few years, the jurisdiction of those commissions which did not already have it was extended to street railways and gas, electric, and telephone and telegraph companies. People had talked about these reforms for many years. The disclosures of corruption in 1905 and 1906 catalyzed their enactment and set off a fundamental transformation of the functions of state governments.

The origins and nature of state progressivism had much in common everywhere, but there were crucial differences of circumstance and detail. In the South, progressivism was deeply and inherently racist and was also, if anything, more broadly and passionately felt than elsewhere in the nation. These two characterizations are not contradictory. Every state of the old Confederacy took action to exclude blacks (and some whites) from the ballot by legal or constitutional means, or both. This process had begun in the 1870s, but the crucial disfranchising years were those from 1890 to 1908. In the same period, the cities and states of the South enacted "Jim-Crow" segregation laws which relegated blacks to separate and inferior public services and allowed their exclusion from private facilities such as theaters, nonpublic schools, restaurants, and hotels. Most southern whites approved these measures and considered them to be, if not "progressive" in themselves, at least essential to progressivism for whites.

Race had obsessed southern politics since Reconstruction, and, during the Populist 1890s, wealthy whites caught a glimpse of the dangers which awaited them if poor whites and blacks ever succeeded in cooperating politically. But if blacks were excluded from politics, whites could then safely disagree among themselves about social or economic matters. With the race problem thus "settled," white Southerners turned to other serious troubles of their impoverished region. A historic ideology of opposition to privilege and power—which had been familiar in the South since the days of Andrew Jackson and which the Populists of the 1890s had passionately voiced—set the tone of progressivism there. The urban, business-minded elements who assumed the leadership of southern progressivism restrained the application of these ideas, but a profound egalitarianism (for whites) ran deep in the region. There was, after all, so much to be done to bring the South out of isolation, ignorance, and poverty. Now the region caught up—in rewriting election laws, regulating corporations, taxing railroads, improving schools, and reforming city governments. Other regions sometimes found themselves following the South's lead in these areas during the progressive era.

As in the South, progressivism in the North Central and Plains states and the Far West borrowed from, although it was not confined by, the Populist heritage. Rural elements gave progressive candidates, such as La Follette and Cummins, crucial support, and the problems of the farmer shaped much of the progressive agenda. Western reform also grew out of long-standing factional cleavages in many state Republican parties. After 1900, the "outs" proved remarkably adept in using anticorporation and antimachine rhetoric to displace the "ins." Some of this was political opportunism, but it could not have succeeded without tapping deeply felt political and economic grievances among the voters. The railroads were the main villains in the western states, although mining and timber corporations and public-utility companies were also targets for reformers. Perhaps the most distinctive aspect of western progressivism was its passion for the more democratic, antiinstitutional political reforms, such as the initiative, the referendum, and the recall, and a form of the direct primary which allowed voters to cross party lines. Not every western state adopted these measures, but they were more common there than anywhere else in the nation.

The Northeast, like the other sections of the country, showed many faces of progressivism, but there were distinctive features of reform also in that region. Eastern progressivism tended to focus on urban problems and to be both more conservative and somewhat less passionately felt than in the South and West. Without roots in either Populism or long-standing party factionalism, it drew on diverse, often conflicting, sources. Urban, foreign-stock reformers gave decisive support to the progressives' social-reform causes, while old-stock reformers tended to be the key proponents of change in the election laws. In several eastern states, particularly Massachusetts, progressivism built on a long tradition of governmental activism and sometimes refined and extended well-established policies. Yet in the East, too, progressivism was a major political force. It changed the nature of political participation and state government there as much as in the West and South.

PROGRESSIVISM
MOVES TO WASHINGTON

Progressivism moved dramatically onto the national stage in 1905 and 1906 as a consequence of a growing awareness that only the federal government was capable of solving the problems of a continental nation. During Theodore Roosevelt's second term (1905–1909), progressivism embarked on this new and larger task.

Roosevelt was a lifelong Republican politician, but an uncommon one. The fact that he had entered politics at all in the early 1880s was unusual for a young man of his wealth and background. Yet he wanted, as he later wrote in his *Autobiography* (1913), to be a member of the "governing class," and he plunged into the maelstrom of New York City's politics almost as soon as he was graduated from Harvard. By 1901, he had behind him twenty years of public service in city, state, and national government.

Throughout his political apprenticeship, Roosevelt had depended for advancement more upon his own energy and capacity for self-advertisement than upon the regular Republican organization. Long before the famous charge up Kettle Hill during the Spanish-American War, Roosevelt had become an American celebrity. His flamboyant moralism made good newspaper copy, and his great, gleaming teeth and prominent eye-glasses were wonderful cartoon material. As a result, Roosevelt felt less need for the party than almost any other politician of his day. Throughout his life, whenever he spoke of the value of political parties, he did so with moderation. Republican professionals did not savor Roosevelt's independence and his seeming emotionalism, but they recognized his political skills. Actually, Roosevelt had superlative control over his emotions; he used them shrewdly to win the abundance of affection which his friends and countrymen showered upon him. As early as the 1880s, some acquaintances had predicted that this unusual man would someday be President of the United States. It seems fair to speculate that young Theodore thought of this, too.

In his politics, Roosevelt was simultaneously a conservative and a progressive. He was frank to say that American economic institutions could best be protected from socialism through moderate, ameliorative changes which made life more decent for working people. His progressivism was thus pragmatic and calculating; it sprang, not from a deep and instinctive sympathy for the poor, but from a hard-headed realism. (As one of his biographers has said, Roosevelt was not a compassionate man.) He reserved his most caustic criticism, not for radicals, but for blind business magnates who defended the status quo against all reform whatever. Such men, Roosevelt believed, were fools who risked a revolution without knowing it.

Two of Roosevelt's contributions to national progressivism stand out. First, he inspired public opinion and guided it toward reform. Roosevelt rarely, if ever, originated a progressive measure, but he had a keen sense for timely ideas. He was also fully aware of the intense interest and curiosity which he aroused and of the immense potential power of his high office. Thus he vitalized issues, stimulated discussion, and brought people around to his point of view. He was better, on the whole, in dealing with the public than with the leaders of Congress. Roosevelt could persuade others because he was always so obviously convinced that he was right. People responded to his certitude and moralism. Consequently, public opinion grew in importance as an independent political force during Roosevelt's presidency.

Roosevelt's second great progressive achievement was the creation of administrative government as an antidote to social conflict. Nineteenth-century Republicans had tended to deny and disguise economic and social differences; Roosevelt frankly acknowledged them. He quickly added, however, that the government could reduce conflict through efficient administrative action. If the facts were gathered and expertise applied, decisions could be reached and programs carried out which would benefit every group. Conservation, a cause to which Roosevelt was devoted, is a good case in point. The problem of the management of natural resources was essentially one of reconciling the conflicting needs of the different users of the nation's forests, waters, and minerals. Administrative agencies staffed by experts, Roosevelt believed, would make rational choices satisfactory to everyone. In other areas, too, he supported the establishment of administrative boards and commissions to perform the federal government's growing functions. He also tried to impose efficient standards of operation on existing public agencies.

These two contributions alone mark Roosevelt as the most creative politician of the early twentieth century. The invigoration of independent public opinion and the creation of administrative government lay at the heart of progressivism. They were also among the most important elements of the transformation of politics and government which progressivism accomplished, not only in Washington, but across the country.

The most pressing question which Roosevelt faced was what to do about the "trusts." Rapid business consolidation had aroused widespread demands for some kind of governmental action, and Roosevelt came forward with not one, but three solutions: publicity, trust busting, and regulation. Publicity involved the exposure of the harmful practices of big business and then reliance upon public pressure to stop the questionable behavior. Roosevelt had advocated this approach while he was Governor of New York (1899–1900); as President he urged—and got—the creation of the Bureau of Corporations in 1903 for just this purpose. But publicity turned out to be too mild an approach. Trust busting was a more aggressive tactic. During Roosevelt's two terms as President, the Justice Department filed forty-three cases under the Sherman Antitrust Act either to restrain or dissolve monopolistic business combinations; they included the so-called Beef Trust, the Northern Securities Company, the Standard Oil Company, and the American Tobacco Company. Roosevelt considered these suits necessary both to dramatize the issue and to establish the federal government's authority over big business, but he really lacked confidence in the idea of smashing corporations. Gradually, he turned to the ongoing administrative regulation of company practices as the best governmental means for dealing with big business.

Roosevelt was keenly sensitive to the nationwide outcry against corrupt corporations and devoted much of his second term to measures for the regulation of business. His own first priority, announced a month after his reelection in 1904, was to give the Interstate Commerce Commission (ICC) power effectively to control the railroads. Although Roosevelt probably would have been content with the passage of this one regulatory measure, startling public events and the disclosures of muckraking journalists focused attention on other industries which also seemed to require federal supervision: meat packing, food processing, and drug manufacturing. In each instance, a combination of investigative reporting and a campaign of action by professionals (doctors, pharmacists, and chemists) dramatized intolerable conditions and set off a clamor for reform. In Congress, the debate over the measures always came down to details. Who would pay for regulation? Should the government set rates? Could the courts overturn a commission's decision? Roosevelt worked for compromises on these and other questions, and he won three major regulatory measures in 1906: the Hepburn Act, which strengthened the ICC and gave it the power to set maximum railroad rates; a Pure Food and Drug Act; and a Meat Inspection Act.

During his final two years in the White House, Roosevelt went beyond the idea of regulation to advance the most far-reaching federal economic and social program in American history to that time. Among other things, he proposed measures for the federal incorporation of all corporations doing business across state lines, income and estate taxes, restrictions on the use of court injunctions against strikers, an employers' liability law to protect injured workingmen, and a stronger eight-hour law for federal employees. Congress balked at all these proposals. The regular Republicans (the Old Guard) still dominated the legislative branch, and they opposed Roosevelt's expansion of presidential power at their expense and profoundly objected to his proposals for further federal regulation. Regular Republicans were accustomed to promoting, not restraining, business.

Even as Roosevelt was seeking new programs, a growing bloc of midwestern Republican dissidents—or "insurgents" as they were beginning to be called—was pressing for still stronger measures of regulation and social justice. Having captured their own states, insurgent leaders such as La Follette of Wisconsin, Cummins of Iowa, and Joseph H. Bristow of Kansas moved on to Washington where they constituted a potent force in both houses of Congress. They believed that the protective tariff was the "mother of the trusts" and that, if protection was eliminated on trust-made goods, the behemoths of business would be destroyed by competition. Although this was, in some respects, a proposal to benefit midwestern consumers at the expense of eastern producers, it was a fundamental challenge to a historic Republican doctrine, and the insurgents infused a genuinely felt moral appeal into their demand for reform of the tariff law. Unlike the Old Guard, the insurgents had the good luck to be able to push the nation in the direction in which it was going anyway, and also to help themselves and their constituents in the process.

If Roosevelt had remained in the White House, he might well have been able to hold together the rapidly disintegrating Republican party. Instead, he kept his promise to retire after a second term and chose Secretary of War William Howard Taft of Ohio as his successor. Taft easily defeated William Jennings Bryan in the autumn of 1908. The new President was obese and often indolent; in temperament he was more inclined to act the part of a disinterested judge than an engaged politician. Taft gave lip service to Rooseveltian progressivism, but his instincts led him back to the party regulars. In 1909, he called a special session of Congress to lower the tariff. When a measure emerged which gave manufacturers almost as much protection as ever, Taft infuriated midwestern insurgents by saying that it was the best tariff law that the Republican party had ever enacted. Only in the area of federal policies toward business did the Taft administration seem progressive, although, compared to Roosevelt, Taft placed more emphasis on trust busting than on regulation.

Taft's problems were complicated by the emergence of many nonpartisan political organizations determined to shape policy. Such groups, which had always been active in American politics, had become more important than ever after the 1890s. By the time of Taft's administration, they were enormously potent. Many of the organizations represented business and commercial interests; during the tariff debate of 1909, for example, they lobbied unceasingly and successfully for favorable treatment. Organized labor, too, was by now deeply involved in national politics. Beginning in 1906, the AFL had moved toward cooperation with the Democratic party, and their cautious alliance grew stronger in succeding years. Self-styled reform associations of all sorts were also making their opinions heard in state and national politics. The cause of woman suffrage, stalled since the 1890s, now regained momentum through the efforts of the National American Woman Suffrage Association (NAWSA). In 1910, several states granted women the vote, and more states followed over the next few years. Social-justice organizations, which called for the protection of working women and children, also moved energetically into politics during this period.

While progressive reform organizations flourished, a significant third party reached a peak of strength during the Taft presidency. The Socialist Party of America, led by Eugene V. Debs, who had gone to jail after the Pullman strike in 1894 and come out a radical, had 58,000 members by 1908 and more than twice that number four years later. On election days, its strength was far greater than that, and by 1912 some 1,000 Socialists held office in thirty-three states and 160 cities. Milwaukee elected a Socialist mayor in 1910, as did more than seventy towns and cities during the following year. The Socialist party was often accused of being dominated by foreigners, but it actually promoted a homemade brand of socialism. Most of its members (if not voters) were native-born. In Oklahoma, the banner Socialist state in 1912, socialism bore a strong cultural and political resemblance to Populism. In Milwaukee, reform-minded Socialists under Victor L. Berger cooperated closely with the city's labor unions and used the same type of ethnic appeals in which American parties had always specialized. On the lower East Side of New York, the Socialists ran best when they, too, recognized the cultural identities of their Russian and German-Jewish supporters. To be sure, the Socialists did advocate and defend radical economic policies. They were doing so very successfully when an even stronger third party, the Progressives, appeared on the scene in 1912.

In that year the political strains which had been accumulating since 1905 turned a presidential election into the climactic battle of the progressive era. The stage was set for such a contest by the division of the GOP into warring progressive and conservative wings. The split, visible as early as Roosevelt's second term, had widened during the tariff debate of 1909, and it became more gaping in the off-year elections of 1910. In that year, Roosevelt had returned from an African safari and triumphant European tour and plunged back into politics on an advanced progressive platform of the regulation of business, social justice, and direct democracy, which he called the New Nationalism. President Taft, now estranged from Roosevelt, tried to prevent the renomination of the Republican congressional insurgents who supported the New Nationalism. For his efforts, Taft suffered a double defeat in 1910: the insurgents survived, and the Democrats captured the House of Representatives. Then in 1911 and 1912, the Republican breach widened even more. Through a dozen bitter presidential primaries (the first ever held) in the spring of 1912, Roosevelt and Taft fought it out for their party's nomination. Roosevelt won most of the primaries, but a convention controlled by the Old Guard narrowly renominated Taft. Roosevelt and his supporters walked out. Joined by a prominent group of social reformers, they met later in an emotional convention of their own, formed the Progressive (Bull Moose) party, and nominated Roosevelt for President. The Democrats, meanwhile, sensing victory, took forty-six ballots to choose Governor Woodrow Wilson of New Jersey as the man to capitalize on the division in the Republican party.

Wilson's nomination gave the Democrats an opportunity to put behind them almost two decades of demoralization and disorganization. The party had never really reunited after the bitter sectional and ideological divisions of the 1890s or recovered from Bryan's two losses to McKinley in 1896 and 1900. The Great Commoner, defeated a third time for President in 1908, had remained the party's titular leader because no national Democratic figure commanded enough strength to displace him. But Bryan never had been able to extend his own base beyond rural and small-town America into the cities where a different, immigrant-based Democratic party was located. Even more than the Republicans, the Democrats had trouble bringing their party doctrines into line with twentieth-century realities. Weak government and state rights still struck a strong emotional chord among many Democrats. The Democrats' growing alliance with organized labor was one sign that the party could deal with the new interest-group politics, and their capture of the House of Representatives in 1910 proved that the Democracy, in spite of all its incongruities, at least had survived as a major party. Even so, it was Wilson's task to unite the Democracy in 1912 and then, if elected, to undertake the much harder task of turning slogans into legislation.

Compared to Eugene Debs' Socialist program, on the one hand, and Taft's conservative Republican platform, on the other, the Bull Moose Roosevelt and the Democrat Wilson both looked like moderate candidates near the progressive middle of the nation's ideological spectrum. There were, nonetheless, real differences of emphasis and policy between the two reformist nominees of 1912. Their divergent appeals gave the nation its fullest opportunity to decide what progressivism meant. Roosevelt's platform constituted a remarkable compendium of almost every social and political reform then talked about in the United States—all bound together by one of the boldest visions in the history of mainstream American politics. The vision was that of a collective democratic society presided over by a strong federal government to regulate and protect every interest. Significantly, the Progressive platform said scarcely anything about busting trusts but instead declared that the concentration of modern business was both "inevitable and necessary." Adopted at the urging of many of Roosevelt's business backers over the opposition of insurgent Republicans, the platform expressed the tenets of what is sometimes called the "corporate liberal state": big government working in harmony with big economic interests to regulate corporations, guarantee the rights of labor, and protect the weak.

The Democratic program in 1912 was less comprehensive and less bold than Roosevelt's, but it was strikingly suited to accomplish Wilson's main task. While declaring that he and his party were the true progressives, Wilson still managed to sound the traditional Democratic themes of state rights and small government. The key to his frankly ambiguous program was the concept of the New Freedom. Crafted by Louis D. Brandeis, the crusading lawyer of Boston, as an alternative to Roosevelt's collectivist New Nationalism, the New Freedom proposed to restore the conditions of economic competition and equality of opportunity which had existed in the past but without permitting the federal government to become as big or as paternalistic as Roosevelt wanted. "Free men need no guardians," Wilson intoned, and he warned that a big paternalistic government would inevitably be controlled by big businessmen.

The results of the election of 1912 revealed that Wilson had succeeded in holding his party together and in preventing Roosevelt from uniting the progressive forces. Even with only 42 per cent of the popular vote, Wilson ran well ahead of Roosevelt (27 per cent) and Taft (23 per cent) and carried forty out of the forty-eight states. The Socialist Debs won 6 per cent of the popular total, most of it in the West. Allan Lichtman and Jack B. Lord II have estimated that Wilson won the support of 83 per cent of those persons who had voted for Bryan in 1908, while Taft and Roosevelt won, respectively, 40 per cent and 46 per cent of the ballots cast for Taft in 1908 (see below, p. 130). One major party thus stayed together, while the other one divided into two approximately equal parts. In several respects, the election of 1912 was the first "modern" presidential contest in American history. The use of direct primaries, the challenge to traditional party loyalties, the candidates' issue orientation, and the prevalence of interest-group political activities all make the election of 1912 look more like that of 1980 than that of 1896.

The man who went to the White House in 1913 had, in a sense, been preparing all his life for the presidency. Even as a young man, Wilson had admired—and, in his mind, imitated— the leaders of the British Parliament, William E. Gladstone in particular. Wilson dreamed of becoming the brilliant orator who led a party based on principles. His first book, *Congressional Government* (1885), was a harsh analysis of the congressional committees which dominated the government of the United States and yet operated utterly beyond the bounds of responsibility. Wilson favored what later came to be called "responsible party government": the election of strong executive leaders who would be held accountable for redeeming party pledges. As President of the United States from 1913 to 1921, Wilson tried to be such a leader.

Despite his preparation for high office, Wilson—unlike Roosevelt—was before 1910 an unlikely candidate to achieve the presidency, especially as a progressive. He was a Southerner, born in Virginia, and no Southerner had occupied the White House since Andrew Johnson. Wilson, moreover, was not a politician at all until he was fifty-three years old but successively a lawyer, college professor, and university president. Along the way, he was an ivory-tower advocate of conservative political doctrines. All this changed in 1910. Catapulted into office as Governor of New Jersey under the sponsorship of the state's Democratic boss, who hoped to benefit from his nominee's respectability, Wilson boldly seized the opportunity for leadership. In 1911, he put through the legislature a comprehensive program of political and economic reforms which transformed New Jersey into a model progressive state and made Wilson a logical candidate for President. His ideological metamorphosis had been relatively quick, however, and Wilson only slowly deepened his understanding of progressivism, whose national leader he now became with his election to the White House.

To that role Wilson brought formidable strengths but also some important weaknesses. He had the ability to articulate in moving terms the high ideals of economic and social justice for which the progressives stood. Wilson knew, moreover, how to fill the part of the strong executive at just the time when the executive branch was becoming the center of the national government. Above all, he proved to be what he had dreamed of becoming—a commanding leader of his party, able to inspire the Democrats in Congress and unite them behind a common program. This last achievement is particularly remarkable when one considers how little practical political experience Wilson had had and in what low esteem party loyalty was held by many people in the progressive era. Wilson's liabilities lay in his excessive moralism, self-righteousness, partisanship, and tendency to trust his own judgment and that of a small coterie of advisers. These weaknesses became more pronounced during his second term as President. Wilson was inspiring in oratory—his speeches literally changed the course of history—but he did not seek the adulation of the masses. Compared to Roosevelt, he was perhaps more admired yet certainly less loved. Even so, Wilson left a record of reform from 1913 to 1920 which surpassed Roosevelt's. Political progressivism, however we define it, found fulfillment and reached its apogee under Woodrow Wilson.

Wilson's original conception of reform was limited and traditional. It amounted to curtailing special privileges for business by breaking up the worst trusts, by lowering the protective tariff, and by reforming the banking and currency systems in order to make capital available to the small entrepreneur. Critics had noted in 1912 that, although Wilson's diagnosis of the nation's ills was insightfully broad, the remedies which he offered under the name of the New Freedom were strikingly cautious. Once in office, Wilson at first resisted and then slowly accepted an expanded progressive program. His early years as President coincided with the peak of the nationwide ferment for reform. Spurred by the new Progressive party, by hundreds of local and national progressive organizations, and by an articulate and growing body of left-wing and radical thinkers, Wilson encouraged—indeed, helped to focus—

the new popular mood. By 1916 he had put through a program of economic regulation and social reform which looked more like the New Nationalism than the New Freedom.

In just two years, Wilson's administration revamped the federal government's economic role. The Underwood-Simmons Act of 1913 eliminated or substantially reduced tariff duties on raw materials and manufactured goods and imposed a small but graduated tax on personal incomes. Late in the same year, the Federal Reserve Act restructured the nation's banking and currency system for the first time since the Civil War. The measure created twelve Federal Reserve banks to perform central banking functions and issue currency for member banks in their districts. It also created a Federal Reserve Board, publicly controlled, to administer the Federal Reserve System. The Federal Reserve Act reflected a series of compromises between large and small banking interests and between different regions of the nation. In getting these two measures enacted, Wilson was at his best as a party leader as he pressured and cajoled Democrats in Congress, assailed lobbyists, and orchestrated the give and take of legislative details.

While the tariff and banking acts exemplified Wilson's original understanding of reform, his administration's response to the problem of the trusts in 1914 took him closer to a Rooseveltian solution. Wilson at first simply favored a stronger antitrust law, embodied in the so-called Clayton bill, together with a companion measure which created an interstate trade commission with fact-finding authority but no powers of enforcement. Pressured, however, by a diversity of interests, including businessmen as well as progressives, Wilson ultimately went along with the creation of the Federal Trade Commission (FTC), a permanent agency with strong powers to prevent the suppression of competition. The Clayton antitrust bill became law, too, but in slightly weakened form. Wilson had come around to the position that only continuous federal regulation could solve the problems posed by big business. He had come to hope, as well, that the FTC's creation would inaugurate, not an era of confrontation between business and government, but one of harmony and handsome cooperation. That had been precisely the aim of Roosevelt and his big-business backers in 1912.

In contrast to his bold leadership in economic legislation, Wilson moved more cautiously for social reform. His early failure to support federal child-labor legislation (the single most popular social reform of the time) displeased progressives, while his policy of sanctioning the racial segregation of some federal offices angered reformers concerned with justice toward black citizens. However, by 1916 Wilson was supporting a number of social reforms which he earlier had opposed or refused to support, including a federal child-labor law, a workmen's compensation measure, an agricultural credits act, and woman suffrage. Wilson also pushed through measures for federal aid to education, to agricultural extension, and to highway construction. Changing personal convictions certainly were the major factor in Wilson's conversion to advanced progressivism, but his need for the support of former Progressive voters, whose party had collapsed in 1916, also helps to account for the torrent of social-reform measures which he signed in the months before that year's presidential election. All told, by the time that he won reelection, Wilson's administration had enacted the most extensive program of social and economic legislation in United States history before 1933. More than that, his first term brought to a climax a decade in which American politics and government at every level were transformed even more profoundly than they would be by the New Deal.

THE DECLINE OF PARTIES AND THE RISE OF INTEREST GROUPS

Such were some of the leading political events at each level of government during the early 1900s. Let us now evaluate them and see their relationship to progressive reform. Much of what occurred during this period contributed to a profound and enduring change in the nature of mass political participation. Innumerable laws redefined the eligible electorate by excluding some people from voting and including others. Even electors whose eligibility remained unchanged found that the new laws had altered the rules, and even the purpose, of voting. The progressives tended to describe these reforms as efforts to purify democracy by curtailing corruption, weakening party bosses, and restoring power to ordinary people. Some of these stated goals were partially achieved, but the reformers' democratic rhetoric is far too self-serving to be taken at face value. Nearly every election-law reform contained fundamental ambiguities— even such seemingly straightforward ones as black disfran- chisement and woman suffrage—and many of the laws produced results which surprised at least some of their advocates.

On the whole, party voting became a less important form of political participation during the progressive era than during the nineteenth century. At the same time, as we will see, other types of political influence assumed new significance. Interest- group activity became for many people a permanent means of affecting government. For even more Americans, that amorphous but crucial entity, "public opinion," offered an indirect avenue of political influence. These newer methods of expression by no means directly replaced voting. Certain groups gained in power, while others lost as a result of the transformation of political participation. In some cases, it is hard to say who came out ahead and who suffered. These ambiguities suggest the complex- ity of the transition from nineteenth- to twentieth-century politics which progressivism helped to effect.

Many of the new rules were directed against the party machines. There had always been distrust of parties, even during the nineteenth century. But such distrust assumed great potency in the early 1900s. The major parties seemed outmoded. Their historic ideologies were far less relevant to an urban- industrial society which demanded active governmental inter- ventions than to a nineteenth-century nation where discrete policies of economic promotion constituted most of the gov- ernment's work. Special-interest organizations found the major parties too diffuse to meet their needs. Almost every cultural, as well as every economic, group resented what they considered to be the overrepresentation in the major parties of people whom they abhorred. These related developments contributed to elevating what had been a minor theme during the nineteenth century into a major progressive objective—the weakening or, if possible, the destruction of the party machines.

Nowhere was the impulse to accomplish this goal greater than in the large cities. Well before 1900, diverse groups of urban citizens complained about the irrelevance of the national parties to the housekeeping tasks of municipal government. By the 1890s, middle- and upper-class reformers had fashioned a well-developed critique of the machines for the high real-estate taxes which they imposed, the corruption which they practiced, and, above all, the special attentions which they lavished on the poor, immigrant voters who formed the base of the bosses' electoral support. Samuel P. Hays and others have suggested that the structural reforms discussed above were intended to take power not simply from the parties but, even more, from the lower-class voters whom the machines served ("The Politics of Reform in Municipal Government in the Progressive Era").

But the urban reforms of the progressive era were more complicated than the Hays thesis suggests. For one thing, city elites by no means always agreed among themselves on what constituted desirable forms of politics and government. David C. Hammack's *Power and Society: Greater New York at the Turn of the Century* (1982) and Carl V. Harris' *Political Power in Birminghan, 1871–1921* (1977) suggest this complexity. Whenever such subjects as taxes, regulation, and municipal services came up for debate and decision, each urban elite had its own conception of what should be done and who should pay for it. Some wealthy groups were closely tied to the party organizations, and so they opposed the antimachine reforms which other elites supported. Even if reformers could agree on a measure such as commission government, moreover, the actual results often proved surprising. In Jersey City, for example, the Democratic machine strenuously opposed the adoption of commission government, while the city's businessmen supported it. But once approved in 1913, the new form of government became the very basis of Boss Frank Hague's rule of that city for three decades. In general, urban party machines proved hard to eradicate, and many elites made their peace with the bosses, just as they had done in the nineteenth century.

Overall, there is no reason to say that the reformed city governments of the progressive era were inherently any less democratic than their predecessors. There is too much hard evidence of partisan corruption and mismanagement to warrant the contention that reform was simply one social class's effort to take power from another. Often municipal reform crusades received considerable support in the tenement districts; in many instances the reformers could not have won otherwise. This is not to say that the urban progressives of the early 1900s changed the rules of politics without a consciousness of class interests. In the cities, as elsewhere, each group of reformers inevitably emphasized its own, often selfish, vision of how to bring politics into line with urban-industrial realities.

Outside the cities, too, many of the most important election-law reforms of the progressive era struck at the party machines and their methods. One significant series of changes drastically revised and regulated the ways in which the parties made their nominations and conducted elections. For much of the nineteenth century, parties had been largely untouched by the law. They chose their candidates, printed and distributed their ballots (known as tickets), and got out the vote pretty much as they chose. Then, beginning around 1890, laws passed in almost every state converted the parties from private into public organizations. The first—and, in some ways, most important—of these was the secret, publicly printed Australian ballot, which listed every candidate of every party. The new ballot was adopted in most states within a few years after the scandal-ridden presidential election of 1888. Since it was available only at the polls and cast in secret, it made it much more difficult for a vote-buying party boss to know that the "goods" had been delivered. Reformers welcomed the Australian ballot and hailed it as a remedy for the worst kind of political corruption.

The new ballot, however, did much more than curtail a particular form of corruption. It required the individual voter to read, interpret, and mark his own ballot, instead of just cast the old party ticket. The Australian ballot thus discouraged persons not literate in English from voting at all. Some of the new ballot's supporters were well aware of this effect. Australian-ballot laws also could hurt third parties by imposing stringent requirements for placing their candidates on the ballot or by prohibiting the "fusion" slates of a weaker major party and a third party. Peter Argersinger has shown that the Republicans used such ballot-law requirements to undermine cooperation between the Democrats and Populists in many western states ("'A Place on the Ballot': Fusion Politics and Antifusion Laws," *American Historical Review,* 1980). These laws, he has demonstrated, significantly contributed to the collapse of the Populist party.

Of even more importance in the long run, the Australian ballot caused states to become involved in the regulation of party nominations. If the government printed the ballots, there would have to be some official way to determine which parties and whose names were to be placed upon them. This necessity, together with the continuing outcry against the corruption of the nominating process by boss-dominated party conventions, brought about the passage of laws, first to regulate the conduct of party conventions (the indirect primary) and then to establish direct primaries in which party members themselves selected the nominees.

Many motives lay behind the rapid adoption of the direct primary. In the Democratic South, where state laws permitted the parties to determine their own membership qualifications, the dominant party's direct primary became an all white primary. Even where blacks continued to vote in general elections, they were denied a voice in selecting the almost certainly victorious Democratic nominees. Southern supporters of the direct primary of course intended it that way. In the Midwest, the direct primary often was an instrumentality which one Republican faction used to displace another. The continued success of the La Follette machine in Wisconsin rested in large part on direct nominations. Almost everywhere, the direct primary received impetus from the outcry against corrupt alliances between party machines and business corporations.

In practice, the direct primary fulfilled some of its supporters' expectations and confounded others. It eliminated the most blatant abuses of the machine's control over convention nominations, but it left the party leaders in substantial control of the selection of candidates. Participation in primary elections tended to be relatively low, and only in rare circumstances did the masses of voters rise up to defeat the leaders' chosen nominees. In states dominated by one party (as most were in the early 1900s), the majority party's primary contest effectively decided the general election. This placed the choice of officials in the hands of a minority of voters and caused the further atrophy of the lesser major party. Some political scientists have concluded that the direct primary may have weakened rather than strengthened popular control over elected officials.

State governments in the progressive era also began strictly to regulate campaign methods and finances. So-called corrupt practices acts, passed in the 1890s and early 1900s, clamped down on many of the old techniques which parties had used to arouse their supporters and get them to the polls. The old practice of compensating loyal voters for their time on election day by the payment of a couple of dollars, or of simply buying votes, was sharply curtailed. So was the availability of campaign funds for this and other purposes, since corporate donations now were outlawed. These measures contributed to the decline of the hoopla and excitement, as well as of the high levels of participation, which had characterized nineteenth-century elections.

All told, the major political parties emerged from the era of reform less popular and more carefully regulated than before, but also, paradoxically, more firmly embedded in the legal machinery of elections than they ever had been. For third parties, the reforms were damaging. Strict laws made it difficult for any but Democrats or Republicans to get on the ballot, while other measures restricted the political participation of many electors who might well have been among the most likely to cast third-party tickets. These reforms which affected parties were not adopted in a political vacuum. Widely shared popular attitudes, as well as legal enactments, contributed to restraining the major parties from carrying on many of their former activities. Correspondingly, the two largest third parties of the era, the Progressives and the Socialists, waned for reasons which had little to do with the new election laws. Yet those laws took an important, independent toll on the traditional nineteenth-century party politics. Many progressives intended that they should, although the reformers failed to grasp that, in regulating parties, they also were giving them legal status for the first time.

Several progressive election-law reforms curtailed the political power of certain classes of voters, particularly blacks and immigrants. We have discussed the almost complete disfranchisement of blacks in the states of the old Confederacy. In most southern states, black participation after disfranchisement fell to minute proportions and remained insignificant until the 1960s. This result, J. Morgan Kousser has argued in *The Shaping of Southern Politics: Suffrage Restriction and the Establishment of the One-Party South, 1880–1910* (1974), was fully intended by the affluent Democrats who led the drive for disfranchisement and who benefited from the demise of opposition to their regimes. Northern states, too, used some of the same techniques (although far less effectively) to disfranchise immigrants. The secret-ballot law could accomplish this, as could stricter voter-registration requirements. Nine states outside the South passed literacy tests for voting before 1920, and eleven states repealed older laws which permitted aliens to cast ballots once they announced their intention of becoming American citizens.

These frankly restrictive measures had the support of many persons who considered themselves progressives. The reforms which they sought were not intended to enlarge the electorate so much as to "improve" it, to make it more able to fulfill the tasks of citizenship. Each group and class naturally had its own conception of what constituted an improvement, and these conceptions were often racist, nativistic, and elitist. The disfranchisers defended their actions, sometimes sincerely, as means to prevent corruption and set a high standard for political participation. But these reforms also served the purpose of reducing the political power of groups which the progressives considered threatening to the general welfare.

While voting was made more difficult for blacks and immigrants, women won the franchise, first in individual states and then in the nation. Throughout the previous century, women had played political roles—as organizers, petitioners, and speakers on behalf of such causes as antislavery, temperance, women's rights, and Populism. Except in a handful of western states, however, they had been denied the vote. Some states permitted women to participate in school elections and municipal contests, but as late as 1910, only Wyoming, Utah, Colorado, and Idaho gave women full and equal voting privileges. During the second decade of the twentieth century, a combination of strategies enabled women to gain the franchise. The National American Woman Suffrage Association conducted highly organized, well-financed drives for both state suffrage referenda and a national amendment. The association's tactics were moderate, and its campaigns exhibited the familiar progressive attention to organization and education. By 1919 twenty-six states had granted women some form of the vote, and the following year brought complete national success with the adoption of the Nineteenth Amendment. While the NAWSA pursued its moderate strategy, radical suffragists under the leadership of Alice Paul and the National Woman's Party picketed the White House, defied police, got arrested, and made martyrs of themselves by going on hunger strikes when jailed by the authorities. Their tactics, too, contributed to the triumph of woman suffrage.

Like other progressive election-law changes, woman suffrage had its share of ambiguities and ironies. Perhaps the main reason why it took so long for women to win the vote was that suffrage implied that women had interests as individuals, apart from their husbands and children. As Ellen Carol DuBois has observed, such a notion was radically inconsistent with the accepted idea that women's sphere was the family (*Feminism and Suffrage: The Emergence of an Independent Women's Movement in America, 1848-1869,* 1978). Not until the seemingly extreme implications of suffrage were submerged did the reform finally gain widespread acceptance among women as well as men. During the final stages of the drive, suffragists advanced conservative reasons, based on expediency, for giving women the vote. Aileen Kraditor has documented their conservative rationale in *The Ideas of the Woman Suffrage Movement, 1890-1920* (1965). Suffragists argued that the vote would enable women to fulfill their traditional duty to protect the home and would improve the quality of the electorate by increasing the proportion of voters who were white and native-born. A potentially radical reform thus was adopted with conservative implications. In practice, it proved scarcely radical, since women voted less frequently and little differently from men. Yet woman suffrage was an essential reform; it was one of progressivism's greatest achievements.

Overall, the electoral reforms and the accompanying changes in party politics of the progressive era mark it as a political watershed of the first importance in American history. Perhaps only the Jacksonian period—when many of the classic forms of party politics had taken shape—produced a comparable transformation. The percentage of eligible voters who cast ballots declined sharply in all sections of the country after 1900, with women, blacks, and younger voters among the least active. Paul Kleppner and Stephen Baker have shown that younger men and women of immigrant parentage had particularly low rates of voter participation in the early 1900s ("The Impact of Voter Registration Requirements on Electoral Turnout, 1900-16," *Journal of Political and Military Sociology,* 1980). For those who continued to vote, party loyalties counted for less than they had in the nineteenth century; one sign of this was the rise of split-ticket voting around 1904–1906. Election campaigns generally ceased to be rousing affairs based on competing party appeals. Instead, they became calmer, more oriented around special issues, and more easily dominated by charismatic personalities.

Restrictive election laws only partly explain the decline of voter participation and enthusiasm. The progressive era brought a halt to the historic American trend toward universal suffrage and established a countertrend toward making not more but "better" voters. The decline of partisan electoral activity went deeper than the laws, however: it reflected new needs and new beliefs. Parties, even if they were regulated by the states and behaved responsibly, no longer satisfied the political demands of a great many Americans. Those who were not satisfied sought other kinds of influence.

The most effective newer means of political expression after 1900 was interest-group activity. This form of influence gained increased importance in the progressive era and has remained central to American politics ever since. Businessmen were among the most active groups which organized to press their demands upon the government. The National Association of Manufacturers spoke for small businessmen, while the National Civic Federation represented many of the larger industrial and financial concerns. Hundreds of other organizations, which spoke for every size and type of business, went into politics. Workers, too, organized to put pressure on governmental officials for policies which they wanted. The AFL, as we have seen, increasingly cooperated with the national Democratic party, while local unions all over the country used their organized strength to compel attention from state officials. Professional men and women also banded together to get the legislation which they wanted, particularly various forms of governmental recognition of their expertise. Cultural interest groups sought to influence the government for, or against, policies which they wanted, such as the prohibition of alcohol and the restriction of immigration.

Whatever their aims, the new associations used similar

methods: they organized their members, raised money, hired lobbyists, pressured governmental officials, and inundated the public with their propaganda. Most of them found such tactics to be more effective than partisan political activity. The new organizations thus took over many of the political resources— and even the loyalties—which parties had earlier enjoyed.

Interest-group activity gained impetus not only from the dissatisfaction with parties but also from the transformation of governance. As we shall see, , at every governmental level, administrative agencies and commissions came into being to deal with particular economic and social problems. Commonly, the new governmental bodies encouraged close and special contacts with the private groups which they served. Such dealings brought prestige to the commissions and further strengthened the favored associations. In consequence, the new interest system, like the old party system, did not represent everyone equally. Organized social elements performed much more successfully than unorganized ones, and wealthy, educated groups performed best of all.

Public opinion was a subtler type of political influence. Although scarcely new in the progressive era, it achieved fresh potency and found new forms of expression during this period. Politicians such as Theodore Roosevelt, whose strength lay outside the party machines, encouraged and cultivated independent opinion for their own benefit; so did reform organizations and interest groups of all sorts. Nonpartisan newspapers and popular journals, whose numbers and circulation grew significantly in this era, also appealed to—and helped to solidify—public attitudes independent of the parties. Even the parties themselves contributed to the new public opinion through campaign techniques directed at educating the voters, not merely arousing their old loyalties. These related developments brought into being a diffuse but quite potent force which politicians and governmental officials tried to gauge and did not dare to ignore.

Like other forms of political influence, public opinion was weighted toward those who were sufficiently wealthy and organized to articulate and propagate their beliefs. This bias was evident in the uses to which two new formal mechanisms of public opinion were put: the initiative and the referendum. These devices, which permitted voters themselves to propose and enact legislation even against the will of the legislature, were adopted in twenty-two states, mostly in the West, between 1898 and 1918. The initiative and referendum seemingly gave everyone an equal opportunity to change the laws, but in practice they were used most effectively by well-organized interest groups, such as labor unions, prohibitionists, and woman suffragists.

Despite the ironies and disappointments which attended some progressive political reforms, they produced a significant transformation of American politics. Who could compete, the kinds of resources required, and the rewards of participation all changed. One thing remained the same: after 1900, just as before, the political system of the United States was conservative. In both eras the society's poorer elements possessed some political means for making their wants known, but in each era the wealthy had more than their share of power. No one could have imagined or designed the new political system which emerged, but its key features clearly had been sought by many progressives: the regulation of parties, the "improvement" of the electorate, and the legitimation of interest groups. In consequence of these changes, together with the expansion of government, winning offices gave way to influencing policies as the main preoccupation of American politics.

THE TRANSFORMATION OF GOVERNANCE

American government underwent a fundamental transition during the progressive era. Robert H. Wiebe has accurately described it as the emergence of "a government broadly and continuously involved in society's operation" (*The Search for Order*). Both the institutions of governance and the content of policy reflected the change. Where the legislature had been the dominant branch of government at every level, lawmakers now saw their power curtailed by an executive with enlarged power and, even more, by the creation of an essentially new branch of government composed of administrative boards and agencies. Where nineteenth-century policy generally had focused on self-seeking distinct groups and locales, government now began to take explicit account of clashing interests and to assume the responsibility for mitigating their conflicts through regulation, administration, and planning. In 1900, government did very little in the way of recognizing and adjusting group differences. Sixteen years later, innumerable policies committed officials to that formal purpose and provided the bureaucratic structures to achieve it.

In the broadest sense, these governmental changes were the products of the long-term social and economic developments associated with industrialization, urbanization, and immigration. The conflict of group interests, the density of population, and the clash of cultures all called forth demands for authoritative actions to reduce antagonisms and provide the services upon which decent life depended. The United States was not alone in making the transition to a more active state. Indeed, some of the industrialized nations of western Europe were well ahead of the United States in adapting government to new conditions. Many Americans of the early 1900s observed and copied European policies.

Even though the changes in the functions of government were worldwide in scope, the actual nature of the governmental transition in the United States during the progressive era derived from distinctively American attitudes about the state. Ambivalence toward public authority had been a familiar theme in the United States since the eighteenth century. Both individually and collectively, the progressives inherited that ambivalence and showed themselves to be of several minds about the concentration of governmental power. (So, for that matter, did conservatives of the day.) Some reformers abhorred the expansion of government and worked exclusively through private organizations for the changes in which they believed. Most reformers, however, acknowledged, with varying degrees of reluctance, that governmental authority had to be enlarged to deal with economic and social problems. But what should be done, and which officials should do it, were questions which deeply divided progressives.

Amid the disagreements over government, certain elements of a progressive consensus stood out. One was the belief that the legislative branch of government, particularly on the state level, was the least capable and most corrupt branch and ought to be restrained. This attitude was not new to the progressives; many Americans of the 1800s had considered legislators to be partisan, parochial, and selfish men. For almost a century, in consequence, state constitutional revisions had been adopted which lessened the powers of the legislatures. Convinced that the exacting new tasks of government were too demanding for untrained legislators who sat only a few months at a time, the progressives now accelerated this trend toward restricting the powers of the lawmakers. Civil-service regulations limited the patronage at their disposal, while the initiative and referendum forced them to share the job of lawmaking with the people. The Seventeenth Amendment took the selection of United States senators out of the hands of state legislatures.

Perhaps most important, when the government was given new functions to perform, these were not usually entrusted to the legislatures. Instead, it was the executive branch which most enjoyed the confidence of early twentieth-century Americans. Whereas the legislature was inherently fragmented by representatives of antagonistic constituencies, the executive seemed capable of unifying them. As New York's Governor Charles Evans Hughes expressed it in 1910, "Out of the conflicts between competing interests or districts the Executive emerges as the representative of the people as a whole." Hughes himself was one of a new breed of mayors, governors, and Presidents— men such as Tom L. Johnson, Robert M. La Follette, and Theodore Roosevelt—who demonstrated the truth of that statement. Visible and charismatic, they stood above their parties and above any particular economic or social interests. To give such leaders further strength, numerous progressive reforms, adopted at every level of government, enlarged executive authority to make appointments, control the budgetary process, and initiate legislation.

Important as were the innovations which they achieved in the traditional branches, the progressives' most creative changes in the institutions of government came through the establishment of new administrative agencies. Those boards and commissions, staffed with experts and entrusted with significant independent powers of investigation and enforcement, assumed older public functions from the legislature and took on new duties as well. The first of the new bodies—and the ones which paved the way for others—were the regulatory commissions established to supervise the rates and services of utility and transportation corporations. Other types of companies, too, increasingly came under the supervision of commissions. The progressives also utilized independent agencies to make and enforce policy in areas such as business, health, education, labor, taxation, correction, and natural-resource conservation.

Behind the expansion of administrative government lay some characteristic progressive assumptions about public authority and its uses. Where nineteenth-century politicians often had denied and disguised group conflict, the reformers of the early twentieth century not only acknowledged it but also recognized the government's duty to lessen divisions and adjust differences. This could be done, many of them believed, if impartial experts were empowered to gather the facts, analyze them according to the methods of science or social science, and render rational decisions on the basis of their knowledge. Such administrative decisions could fairly take account of the needs of every interest and thus reduce, if not eradicate, the often violent group antagonisms which had frightened Americans of the late nineteenth century.

This was a heady ideal, not altogether fanciful, and sometimes successful. What the reformers frequently failed to recognize, however, was that scientific experts were not necessarily impartial and that interest groups were perfectly capable of dominating administrative agencies. In their ambition to reduce group conflict, moreover, the progressives transferred decision making from the legislative halls to the administrative arena, where unorganized people were often even less likely to make their voices heard. Perhaps most important, the establishment of administrative government created a twentieth-century version of the nineteenth-century illusion that the different interests of an industrial society actually were harmonious. This illusion—that administration would dispel social conflict—was the greatest single flaw in the progressive conception of government.

As the foregoing analysis suggests, the changes in governmental institutions associated with progressivism profoundly affected the scope and content of public policy. Nowhere was this more true than in the economic area. Nineteenth-century economic policies had consisted largely of the distribution of resources and privileges to promote enterprise and industry, with little attention given to weighing the costs against the benefits or to compensating those who were hurt as a result of governmental decisions which benefited others. Regulation of privileged businesses was not unknown, but the enforcement of regulations generally proved minimal. Then, in the early 1900s, what Willard Hurst has called "a new disposition of calculation" entered the policy process (*Law and the Conditions of Freedom in the Nineteenth-Century United States,* 1956). The government scarcely stopped giving things away, but now the allocative decisions came to be supplemented by meaningful measures of regulation and adjustment. To put it another way, the mix of distributive and regulatory policies changed. Many of the most dramatic battles over economic policies during the progressive era—the conservation of natural resources, for example— actually came down to disputes over what the proper mix should be.

Almost everyone who has ever studied early twentieth-century reform has regarded the establishment of effective regulation of business as among progressivism's most distinctive and important achievements. Yet no subject has aroused more controversy among historians of the era than the causes and consequences of regulation. Three quite distinct theories have been put forward: the "public interest" interpretation, the "capture" thesis, and the "pluralist" model (Thomas K. McCraw, "Regulation in America: A Review Article," *Business History Review*, 1975). All three serve to illuminate crucial aspects of the regulation of business in the progressive era.

The public-interest interpretation was the one most frequently given by the reformers themselves and has been echoed by historians sympathetic to them. According to this view, the regulation of business was undertaken to protect the general welfare of the public—and consumers in particular— from the greed and wrongdoing of the corporations. In McCraw's words, "The notion of the 'public interest' . . . dominate[d] the rhetoric of reformers, the utterances of presidents, and the decisions of [regulatory] commissioners." Such rhetoric also engaged the imagination of ordinary Americans during the progressive era. From the time of the discoveries of politico-business corruption in 1905-1906 until at least 1915, when Congress investigated the causes of labor unrest, the nation went through an era of almost continuous investigation and exposure of illicit business practices. The sordid revelations which emerged discredited the practice of granting privileges to corporations and suggested regulation as a much more fitting public policy toward business.

Consumer discontent with rates and services also was expressed in the language of the public interest. Beginning during the depression of the 1890s, cities all across the country experienced outbreaks of consumer anger against utility and transportation corporations. These often led to stricter municipal policies of regulation and supervision. State and federal regulatory measures, too, received impetus from organized consumers outraged by business behavior. In no industry was consumer indignation better illustrated than in that of life insurance, as H. Roger Grant has shown in *Insurance Reform: Consumer Action in the Progressive Era* (1979). The notion of the public interest scarcely explains everyone's motivation for regulation, much less the results of the new policy. But unless due weight is given to the popular passion for protecting the public from rapacious corporations, neither the timing nor the scope and sweep of progressive regulation of business can be understood.

The second theory that accounts for the regulation of business during this time, the capture thesis, almost completely inverts the public-interest interpretation. Not the people, the theory goes, but the regulated businesses themselves were the main beneficiaries of governmental regulation. As stated by Gabriel Kolko (*The Triumph of Conservatism* and *Railroads and Regulation, 1877–1916,* 1965), this second interpretation goes well beyond the contention that the corporations dominated (or captured) the regulatory commissions. Businessmen, Kolko has argued, actually were "the most important single advocates" of federal regulation.

Kolko's evidence makes it clear that some businessmen helped to decide the terms of governmental regulation and sometimes profited from it in practice. But his thesis exaggerates the influence of businessmen. At both the federal and state levels, the origins and consequences of regulation were much more complicated than Kolko acknowledged. Several careful studies of key pieces of national legislation have made such complexity evident. John Braeman's account of the Meat Inspection Act of 1906, for example, has shown that, on a number of important points, the meat packing corporations were defeated in their efforts to determine the details of how the Agriculture Department would supervise their industry ("The Square Deal in Action: A Case Study in the Growth of the 'National Police Power,'" see below, p. 133). Of particular importance, a provision which gave packers the right to appeal the department's decisions to the federal courts was deleted from the final legislation. So, too, was a provision, favored by the packers, which exempted federal meat inspectors from civil-service requirements for a year. In several other instances, Braeman makes plain, the packers indeed got what they wanted from the law. But the shaping of the act as a whole owed less to their influence than Kolko said.

Although Kolko has confined his research to federal legislation, it is important to observe that the origins and results of business regulation by the states also were complex. Studies of several states suggest that the affected industries commonly opposed the adoption of regulatory measures and only later discovered their benefits. Stanley P. Caine's *The Myth of a Progressive Reform: Railroad Regulation in Wisconsin, 1903–1910* (1970) has shown that railroad leaders fought against Governor La Follette's initial proposals for state supervision of their lines. When the arousal of public opinion on the subject seemed to make the passage of such legislation inevitable, however, the railroad men entered the fray, along with other interested groups, and helped to determine the details of the final law. Later, in practice, the railway managers found Wisconsin's railroad commissioners to be sensitive to the needs of their industry. In New York State, too, where major regulatory laws covering public utilities, life-insurance companies, and transportation corporations were passed between 1905 and 1907, industry representatives opposed the measures but later learned to live comfortably with them (Richard L. McCormick, *From Realignment to Reform: Political Change in New York State, 1893–1910,* 1981).

Most recent studies of the regulation of business offer support for the third theory, the pluralist interpretation. According to this view, diverse competing interests—consumers, corporations seeking restraints on their rivals, and the supervised businesses themselves—all had a hand in shaping the details of regulation. None of them typically succeeded in writing everything that they wanted into law, and all found a combination of advantages and disadvantages in the results. Peter Temin's finding that a "welter of competing influences" contributed to the enactment of the Pure Food and Drug Act of 1906 illustrates the pluralist view (*Taking Your Medicine: Drug Regulation in the United States,* 1980). This interpretation is less dramatic than either the public-interest or the capture thesis, both of which pit the people decisively against the businessmen. The pluralist model, in fact, embraces elements of each of the other interpretations. In certain phases of the regulatory process and in particular circumstances, both the public and the corporations proved able to influence, and profit by, governmental supervision.

Over the long run, however, organized economic interests, rather than the unorganized public, tended to benefit most from administrative regulation. The largest groups proved best able to develop close relationships with the new governmental agencies and to make their wants known and understood. Ordinary citizens found it impossible to match the influence of associations with the money and the membership to compel official attention. This result was ironical, but its causes were not conspiratorial. Public outrage against the evils of industrialism was strong enough to set in motion the development of governmental machinery to regulate business corporations but not strong enough, as things turned out, to keep the organized interests from helping to design the machinery and to run it.

By the end of the progressive era, the political and governmental system of the United States was very different from what it had been in the late nineteenth century. It would be hard to say whether the new system was more or less democratic than the old one. Voting had become more difficult for many, but new avenues of popular political influence had opened up. The new agencies of administrative government often bent to the will of the rich, but so had legislative government in the nineteenth century. Probably we will never have a fully satisfactory answer to the question of whether early twentieth-century American politics really became more "progressive" in the casual sense of that word. But we do know a great deal about how particular progressive reforms helped some groups and hurt others. We can also be certain that no one could have anticipated the actual results of political and governmental reform—not the ordinary people, whose outrage against bosses and businessmen gave the era its vitality, nor their enemies either.

THREE

Social Justice
and
Social Control

When Americans of the early 1900s looked at their society, many sensed what a few articulated: the economic changes of the preceding generation had created profound social strains and widespread misery. Mothers worked long hours in unsafe factories in exchange for fewer dollars than single people, let alone families, could survive on in decency. Twelve-year-old children labored there, too; some of them fell down elevator shafts or lost their hands to the machines. Outside the factories in crowded city neighborhoods, violent criminals menaced people and property. In the tenement districts, to which poverty confined the poorest, foreign-born people, both sanitation and personal privacy were rare. In rural America, poverty, ignorance, and simple loneliness were common. These social ills literally made people sick. Venereal disease, tuberculosis, alcoholism, and insanity afflicted great numbers of people; taken into custody by hospitals and asylums, they were seldom cured. Parents, even healthy ones, were unable to protect their children from the dangers of the environment or to perform the whole range of economic and educational functions which families once had filled.

In the early years of the twentieth century, as in every age, those persons who suffered from adversity did what they could to survive and improve their lot. Now, however, they were joined by large numbers of middle- and upper-class reformers. Many of them, inspired by evangelical Protestant beliefs and the Social Gospel, acted out of a heartfelt desire to alleviate suffering and to institute justice. Others sought the professional prestige which they enjoyed as dispensers of scientific solutions for social problems. Most important, as we have said, all progressives were profoundly disturbed by what they perceived as numerous evidences of social disintegration and class conflict.

The fundamental assumption of progressives was their deeply held conviction that men and women were creatures of their environment. Many nineteenth-century reformers had shared the same conviction. But the belief that each person was responsible for his or her own well-being and salvation, and that poverty and failure were caused by weakness of character, was still strong in the late nineteenth century. As industrialization proceeded, however, human interdependence became more obvious than ever before and led intellectuals to challenge the conventional wisdom of individualism. According to R. Jackson Wilson's *In Quest of Community: Social Philosophy in the United States, 1860–1920* (1968), the decline of the ideal of the "transcendent individual" marked a profound change in American culture during the late nineteenth and early twentieth centuries. Thus philosophers such as Josiah Royce and John Dewey, sociologists such as Charles H. Cooley and Edward Alsworth Ross, and Social Gospel ministers such as Walter Rauschenbusch and Washington Gladden all came to believe that people were products of their environments. The conclusion was simple but momentously important.

Many middle-class Americans also saw the point. Men and women who lived in large cities, where social contacts and conflicts were the grist of everyday life, had little choice but to acknowledge their dependence upon each other and to seek common solutions to common problems. Doctors learned that venereal disease and tuberculosis were indices of social conditions; curing them meant stamping out prostitution and eradicating the insanitary conditions that accompanied poverty. Policemen and lawyers saw that crime was most prevalent in certain social environments; the prevention of crime depended on improving the environment and rehabilitating the criminal. Many progressives blamed social ills on the habits and practices of the southern and eastern European immigrants. Reform thus meant restricting immigration, prohibiting the use of alcoholic beverages, and encouraging the Anglo-Saxon way of life. It might even necessitate preventing unfit people from having children. Whatever changes they advocated, progressives tended to recognize the need for solutions which were citywide, statewide, or even nationwide in scope.

As the foregoing suggests, the progressives sought both social justice and social control. Although the relative importance of these two goals is a significant problem in historical interpretation, it is essential to recognize that most progressives pursued both ends. This blending of control with justice was not accidental. Most reformers firmly believed that justice in an industrial society depended on systematic interventions in the lives of people by both private associations and governments. Wrongdoers and deviants had to be restrained; scientific expertise had to be applied to problems; social conflicts had to be mediated. The reformers often disagreed about how much and what kinds of controls were needed. Many of them, moreover, knew that such interventions posed a risk of repression. But it was a chance which they were willing to take because they believed deeply that cohesion, harmony, and justice in modern society depended upon purposeful social planning.

Edward A. Ross' classic study, *Social Control* (1901), provides insight into that conviction. To Ross, a sociologist at the University of Wisconsin, decent life in industrialized society—with "its wolfish struggle for personal success, its crimes, frauds, exploitation, and parasitism"—required restraints or, as he put it, "artificial frames and webs that may hold the social mass together in spite of the rifts and seams that appear in it." Ross' study, which established his national reputation and made "social control" important words in the progressive vocabulary, was a compendium of the diverse "frames and webs" available to social planners. Some of these controls were coercive; that is, they involved the exercise of governmental power and depended on the threat of punishment. Yet Ross preferred a kind of social control which was indirect and self-actuating and which relied upon the persuasion of public opinion, and he feared that even gentle controls endangered individual liberty. "Social control is one means of promoting this welfare," he wrote, "but it is peculiar in that it does so . . . at the expense of that other welfare which is obtained through individual action."

The progressives set about methodically to achieve justice through control. They usually began by organizing a voluntary association. Next they investigated a problem, gathered mountains of data about it, and, finally, analyzed the problem according to the precepts of one of the new social sciences. From such an analysis, a proposed solution would emerge, be popularized through campaigns of education and moral suasion, and—as often as not, if it seemed to work—be taken over by some level of government as a permanent public function.

Certain assumptions guided reformers who used these

methods. One was a belief in the utility of social science for fostering social harmony. Progressives knew very well that different groups in American society had competing interests, and they recognized that conflicting social elements often hurt one another. They were not deluded by a belief in a natural harmony of interests. Yet the social sciences, based as they were on the conviction of social interdependence, offered the possibility that reforms could be devised to harmonize antagonistic social groups. If the facts were gathered and properly understood, solutions could be found which genuinely benefited everyone. Individual reforms might help one group at the expense of another, but a carefully crafted program of reforms would establish such a harmony of interests as so-called natural law could never achieve.

A related progressive assumption was that government could be trusted to carry out broad social reforms. In social policy, just as in the economic arena, nineteenth-century American governments had tended to produce haphazard legislative solutions. What Gerald N. Grob has called "clear policy formation and social planning" were largely absent ("The Political System and Social Policy in the Nineteenth Century: Legacy of the Revolution," *Mid-America,* 1976). Most social progressives did not initially set out to expand the power of government; they placed their confidence in private voluntary organizations. As time passed, however, the reformers increasingly looked to public agencies to execute their programs. Political reform during this period probably contributed to the progressives' confidence in government. More important, the awesome dimensions and interrelatedness of the social problems with which they grappled soon convinced them that only government could establish the comprehensive controls which were necessary to achieve social and economic justice.

The progressives used largely untried methods and acted on assumptions which often approximated mere articles of faith, and it is not surprising that they failed to achieve many of their goals. But they often succeeded, and their fundamental approach to social problems has not yet been repudiated in the

United States. The extent to which the actual achievements of the progressives matched their stated goals varied. To assess their accomplishments, we must take a close look at which people sought which reforms and why they did so.

THE SOCIAL PROGRESSIVES

Early twentieth-century social reform flowed from three wellsprings of thought and motivation. One was the urge felt by certain middle- and upper-class men and women to help make urban life more just, tolerable, and decent. This stream originated in varying combinations of feminism, socialism, and Protestant evangelical fervor and ran most visibly into the settlement-house movement and from there into every conceivable progressive social reform. The second motivation was the drive of trained professionals to apply their knowledge and skills to social problems. The third motivation was the desire of many native-born Americans to use social institutions and the law to restrain and direct the unruly masses, many of whom were foreign-born or black. These three motivations interacted. What distinguished the three impulses toward reform were neither the objects on which they focused nor the methods through which they were expressed. What separated them were the distinctive meanings which they gave to social justice and social control.

In the vanguard of social reform was a remarkable generation of young women and men who founded and ran the settlement houses. Inspired by the example of Toynbee Hall in London, which students from Oxford University established in 1884, many educated sons and daughters of businessmen and professionals moved into city neighborhoods across the United States to live and work among the poor. Their avowed purpose was to reduce class antagonisms—not by dispensing charity, but by educational, cultural, and social activities of every kind and, above all, by establishing close personal relationships in order to break down mutual suspicion between the rich and the poor.

Stanton Coit, an Amherst College graduate who had earned the Ph.D. from the University of Berlin, brought the settlement-house idea to the United States. With a group of reformers, ministers, and labor leaders, Coit settled into the Neighborhood Guild on the lower East Side of New York in 1886. A group of recent graduates of Smith College gathered the next year for a reunion, where they expressed a common desire "to do something concrete to solve social problems." In 1889, together with friends from other women's colleges, they established the College Settlement in a New York tenement area not far from the Neighborhood Guild. (A policeman, thinking that these women were prostitutes, offered to leave them alone in return for a monthly bribe.) Unknown to the founders of the College Settlement, two classmates from Rockford College in Illinois, Jane Addams and Ellen Gates Starr, were just then preparing to settle into Hull-House on South Halsted Street in Chicago. Hundreds of young men and women followed their example. By 1910, there were some 400 settlement houses in cities across the country.

From their bases in the slums, settlement workers provided social and educational services of many kinds. Lectures, art exhibits, pageants, and festivals became the means to awaken poor immigrants to their own cultural heritages and to those of their neighbors. (People of eighteen nationalities lived within the immediate vicinity of Hull-House.) Settlement workers taught classes in homemaking, cooking, sewing, and carpentry; they established nurseries, kindergartens, and employment agencies; and they built playgrounds and founded clubs for groups of every age and sex. They also investigated social conditions and lobbied among municipal officials for services ranging from better garbage collection to the hiring of school nurses. Settlement workers often took the lead in municipal reform campaigns. Through their political efforts, a significant number of programs begun in the settlements became permanent governmental functions.

The men and women who went from colleges to settlement houses did so in part to develop themselves, as well as to serve others. Some were consciously postponing career decisions or marriages. Others went to collect material for their writings. Most were faithful Protestants who sought a way to apply Christian teachings to the social problems of the city. Some were intellectually committed to socialist doctrines. Even though they were influenced by their own class and culture, many settlement workers nonetheless genuinely wished to tear down the barriers of class, race, and religion and to "share the race life," in Jane Addams' words, to get involved in the problems of humanity. The great majority of the settlement workers stayed only a few years, although some, like Addams of Hull-House and Lillian D. Wald of the Henry Street Settlement in New York, stayed a lifetime. "As a group," wrote Allen F. Davis in *Spearheads for Reform: The Social Settlements and the Progressive Movement, 1890–1914* (1967), "they were idealists who believed they were helping to solve the problems of urban and industrial America." They did help, not simply within the settlements themselves but by going forth by the hundreds into progressive crusades of every sort. In Davis' apt phrase, the settlements were indeed the "spearheads for reform."

Women made up a large proportion of the settlement workers, including many of the more innovative ones. Most of them no doubt had many motives in common with their male counterparts, but the women also had distinctive reasons for their actions that were shaped both by the historic experiences of reformers of their sex and by the particular social circumstances in which they found themselves. Female activists in the late nineteenth century had largely concerned themselves with subjects within the "women's sphere" of the home and family. Even when the work of reform took them outside the home, it was mainly to guard domestic morality against such threats as prostitution and alcohol. The agenda of the Woman's Christian Temperance Union (WCTU), the largest women's organization in the late nineteenth-century United States, is a case in point. Under Frances Willard's charismatic leadership, the WCTU had a much wider range of concerns than its name suggests, but most of them fell within women's domain: the establishment of kindergartens, the encouragement of the trade-union movement among women, and the passage of child-labor laws. Most of the early concerns of the settlement-house workers, too, fell well within the "sphere": the conditions of women and children, housing, schools, and playgrounds. As Lois W. Banner has noted in *Women in Modern America: A Brief History* (1974), settlement work "perfectly fitted women's traditional role of service" and so was socially acceptable.

But such work also must have seemed attractive because it offered women the opportunity to move beyond their "sphere." This was not unprecedented. Even the WCTU, observed Carl N. Degler, "raised the consciousness of many women as to their capabilities and potentialities for effective change" (*At Odds: Women and the Family in America from the Revolution to the Present,* 1980). The settlement movement had an even greater ability to do this. There was no aspect of human life to which settlement workers were not exposed, nor any problems utterly beyond their experience. Perhaps more important, as Banner shrewdly wrote of settlement service, "men did not control it." In their work as reformers, these women were relatively free of the constraints of husbands and families.

That settlement women so readily grasped the opportunity to fill unfamiliar roles was due to certain basic changes in the lives and opportunities of women. The long-term decline in the size of the family, the invention of labor-saving household devices, and the gradual absorption by society of many of the family's traditional economic and educational functions gave middle-class wives and mothers more leisure time than they ever had enjoyed before. Of corresponding importance, many more women were attending college. The post–Civil War years had seen the founding of a number of women's colleges, and by 1900 fully 80 per cent of the colleges, universities, and professional schools in the United States accepted women. In 1890, 2,500 women were graduated from college; by 1900, that number had increased to 8,500. Even educated women, however, still found their opportunities for employment extremely limited. While almost no occupation was completely closed to women, the vast majority of female professionals were confined to teaching, nursing, and library work. Marriage generally brought a woman's career to an end, but, by the early 1900s, professional women frequently remained unmarried. Divorce, too, was becoming more common; by 1905, approximately one out of every twelve American marriages broke up. Thus there emerged a growing number of women whose domestic responsibilities were either nonexistent or fewer than their mothers' had been, but who found limited opportunities for employment suited to their educational attainments. For some of these women, settlement work—a profession which they literally helped to invent—offered the chance to do useful work beyond the "sphere."

Such work almost always began with the observation of social facts, or—more rigorously—with the systematic collection of data. This was a progressive obsession, and no one believed in it more completely than did the settlement residents and their social reform allies. One early project at Hull-House was the collection of information on the national origins of everyone who lived in the surrounding area. The results were published in 1895 as *Hull-House Maps and Papers.* More massive compilations of urban facts followed, sometimes produced by the settlements but more commonly prepared by former settlement workers under the auspices of other organizations. Tenement-house conditions inspired some of the most creative data gathering. In 1900, Lawrence Veiller, a "graduate" of University Settlement in New York and now secretary of the tenement-house committee of the Charity Organization Society (COS) of New York, prepared an exhibition designed to show the appalling nature of life in the tenements. The exhibit, termed by Robert H. Bremner "a notable achievement in graphic presentation of sociological data," led Governor Theodore Roosevelt to create a Tenement House Commission (with Veiller as secretary) and to New York State's adoption of a new tenement-house code in 1901 (*From the Depths: The Discovery of Poverty in the United States,* 1956). Many other states copied the New York statute.

The most ambitious progressive endeavor to gather data on city life was the Pittsburgh Survey, sponsored by the newly formed Russell Sage Foundation and conducted by the Charities Publication Committee of the New York COS. The Pittsburgh Survey represented an effort to learn as much as possible about the conditions under which the people of that city lived and worked. Numerous settlement-house residents, including Robert Woods of Andover House in Boston and Florence Kelley, formerly of Hull-House, served as advisers to the persons who conducted the survey. Pittsburgh settlement workers also had a hand in the project. The results, published in six large volumes between 1909 and 1914, showed in what miserable surroundings families lived, how hard men and women labored for little pay, how life-threatening were conditions in the factories, and how rampant were diseases which could have been prevented. Other city surveys and a diversity of reform crusades flowed from the Pittsburgh Survey. Governmental agencies, too, conducted massive investigations of life in America. No such project was more notable than that of the United States Commission on Industrial Relations. Its eleven volumes on the conditions of labor in the United States, published in 1916, constitute an invaluable compendium of facts and progressive analyses.

More than facts came from these studies. They contributed to the social progressives' deepening conviction that poverty was a product of environmental causes, not the result of personal immorality. No book did more to spread this new understanding than *Poverty* (1904) by Robert Hunter, the head worker at University Settlement in New York. Hunter's statistics indicated that 10,000,000 Americans lived below a standard of living necessary for industrial efficiency, and he recommended a comprehensive program of remedial social legislation concerning housing, factories, labor, disease, education, recreation, and immigration. The belief in environmentalism made inevitable the transition from nineteenth-century "charity" to twentieth-century "social welfare" and brought into existence the new profession of social work. Its members, who included many settlement-house graduates, were among the "experts" whose drive to impose their solutions upon society will be considered below. More immediately, the progressives' new-found environmentalism led to efforts to enact the program which Hunter had sketched. If the causes of poverty were social rather than personal, then the solutions would have to be systemwide. And of all systematic remedies, the progressives had the most confidence in legal ones.

The social progressives in the settlement-house tradition put their stamp on various reforms to improve the urban environment. Among the most important were tenement-house reform, the public-playground movement, and a series of comprehensive efforts which soon gained the name of city planning. One approach to the housing problem was the construction of so-called model tenements to encourage the voluntary elimination of the filthiest and most crowded buildings. Increasingly, however, the progressives favored a legal solution—the adoption of stricter housing codes. This was widely achieved, as has been noted earlier, through organization, investigation, and education. But the results did not always match the reformers' hopes. Although enforcement of the codes compelled the elimination of the worst tenements, such laws alone could not bring about the construction of enough decent housing for the poor.

Beginning in 1892, when Hull-House residents established the first public playground in Chicago, the provision of recreational facilities was a high priority of the social progressives. They formed recreation leagues in numerous cities, persuaded municipal authorities to build neighborhood parks, and, in characteristic progressive fashion, established the National Playground Association of America in 1906 to spread the movement across the country. The reallocation of city space for parks inevitably led reformers to a broader view of the need for conscious urban planning. Zoning laws could help to alleviate congestion, revitalize neighborhoods, and instill residents with pride in their city. In time, a new profession emerged from these efforts, but in the beginning, city planning grew out of the spontaneous activity of settlement workers, architects, and well-meaning citizens who believed that poverty was a product of the environment and could be alleviated.

To many reformers, more was at stake than poverty alone. They were also worried about the lifestyles of many urbanites. Drunkenness, prostitution, gambling, the dearth of civic pride, and other forms of "immorality" offended some middle-class progressives quite as much as urban poverty touched their consciences. Fortunately (in the reformers' view), these moral evils could also be to some degree eliminated by improving the environment. Better housing would alleviate the crowded conditions which bred sexual laxity; playgrounds would discourage juvenile delinquency; architectural improvements and a planned environment would promote loyalty to the city. Roy Lubove's *The Progressives and the Slums: Tenement House Reform in New York City, 1890–1917* (1962) has demonstrated that moral concerns weighed heavily on that city's tenement-house reformers. Paul Boyer's *Urban Masses and Moral Order in America, 1820–1920* (1978) has extended a similar interpretation to a much wider range of urban reforms. In Boyer's words, "Social and moral control would depend . . . upon a benign manipulation of the urban environment so as to evoke the desired behavior."

No problem related to poverty touched the socially conscious members of the settlement-house generation as much as did child labor. The campaign to regulate child labor was part of a larger "child-saving" crusade which included efforts to insure germ-free fresh milk, establish juvenile courts, improve recreational facilities, and provide pensions for mothers. The campaign to regulate child labor followed the usual scenario of early twentieth-century reform: investigation, organization, education, and legislation. Early in the 1890s, Florence Kelley of Hull-House had prepared a special report for the Illinois State Bureau of Labor on the conditions of child labor in Chicago's sweatshops. Other investigations followed during the next decade and culminated in the publication of the widely read book, *The Bitter Cry of the Children* (1906), by the Socialist, John Spargo. What these studies revealed was a poignant picture of overworked and underpaid children: uneducated, diseased, poor, and deeply unhappy. Most working children were engaged in agricultural labor, but the worst conditions existed in manufacturing. Southern textile mills, northern canneries, Appalachian coal mines, and tenement sweatshops in northeastern cities were among the worst offenders.

Settlement workers, women's clubs, and local reform groups sought to arouse public opinion against the evils of child labor and to promote remedial legislation. The National Child Labor Committee, established in 1904, spearheaded the crusade. Over the next few years, it experienced considerable success in winning the adoption of state laws which prohibited children from working in certain dangerous jobs, fixed minimum-age limits, and set maximum hours of work. Two thirds of the states enacted some legislation on child labor between 1905 and 1907 alone. But the laws often were full of loopholes—they excluded child labor in the street trades, newsboys for instance—and enforcement proved difficult to accomplish. In textile mills of the South, children as young as twelve were still permitted to work long hours. Seeing the limits of state legislation, the reformers shifted their attention to the federal government. A Children's Bureau, established in the Department of Labor in 1912, gathered more information on the subject, and national legislation in 1916 forbade interstate commerce in goods manufactured by children. Two years later the Supreme Court struck down the law, as it did subsequent similar measures. Even so, child labor continued to decline during the 1920s, in part because the states increased the school-leaving age, in part because new technology made child labor unprofitable.

The problems of working women also aroused social progressives who campaigned for the legal regulation of hours and wages and helped women workers to organize trade unions. Once again, Florence Kelley was a key figure. As a result of her early efforts, the Illinois legislature had passed an eight-hour law for women in 1893, but the supreme court of the state struck it down two years later. Recognizing that legal codes mattered little if public opinion did not support them, Kelley helped to mobilize local consumers' leagues behind a campaign to generate consciousness of the plight of working women and to persuade purchasers not to buy from establishments which treated their employees inhumanely. The National Consumers' League (NCL) organized in 1899, coordinated these local efforts, and Kelley became its general secretary. On the basis of her own research, she published numerous leaflets which demonstrated the ill effects of long hours on the health and safety of women. In response, a number of states enacted laws to restrict the number of hours which women could work.

When Oregon's ten-hour law for women came before the United States Supreme Court in 1908, Kelley, with her close ally and friend, Josephine Goldmark, prepared the statistics and arguments which Louis D. Brandeis (Goldmark's brother-in-law) presented to the court in defense of the measure. The famous "Brandeis Brief" (which Goldmark actually wrote) proved to the Supreme Court's satisfaction that long hours were harmful to the well-being of women. On that basis, the court upheld Oregon's law, and most states enacted women's hours laws during the next decade.

Social progressives encountered greater resistance to the passage of minimum-wage laws for women. The leaders of organized labor—who generally had supported child-labor legislation and women's hours laws—believed that it was better in the long run for workers to win wage increases through collective bargaining and, when necessary, strikes, rather than to accept benefits at the hands of government. It was therefore up to the reformers in organizations such as the NCL to investigate the issue and to mobilize public opinion. This they did. The first volume of the Pittsburgh Survey documented the effects of low wages on women, as did subsequent studies financed by the Russell Sage Foundation. Of most importance was a detailed report on working women prepared (at the urging of settlement-house workers and their allies) by the United States Department of Commerce and Labor and published between 1910 and 1913. Together, these investigations demonstrated the poverty in which working women and their families lived and dramatized how women were driven to prostitution by low wages. As a result, a number of states, beginning in 1912, adopted minimum wage laws for women.

Reformers also helped working women to unionize, and in several key instances they rallied to the side of striking women. Kelley's NCL was active here, but even more important was the Women's Trade Union League (WTUL), an organization which was unique because it brought working-class women into contact with the well-to-do. The WTUL, established in 1903 largely through the efforts of Mary Kenny O'Sullivan and William English Walling—a worker and a rich Socialist intellectual, respectively—succeeded over the years in organizing many female workers, especially in the garment industry. In 1909, when thousands of women in the needle trades in New York went out on strike, members of the New York WTUL joined them on the picket lines, raised money, and mobilized public support. In several subsequent strikes, too, the WTUL brought middle- and upper-class women to the aid of the working women.

One other major type of labor legislation was widely enacted during the progressive era: industrial accident insurance. A number of western European countries had already established systems of compensation for injured workers, but in the United States—where industrial accidents numbered in the hundreds of thousands each year—injured workers (or the families of workers who had been killed) still had to sue for damages in the courts. Under archaic common-law doctrines, they seldom won adequate payments. The alternative to a lawsuit over every case was a plan of compensation under which employers would automatically pay injured workers according to a uniform scale of benefits on the assumption that "industrial accidents are not accidents at all, but normal results of modern industry."

Social progressives played a key role in preparing public opinion for the adoption of workmen's compensation programs. An early volume of the Pittsburgh Survey, *Work Accidents and the Law* (1910), by Crystal Eastman, eloquently marshaled statistics and case studies which showed what great financial (as well as personal) losses workers and their families suffered as a result of industrial accidents. Other progressives and their organizations took up the cause, but the details of the industrial accident plans which most states enacted after 1910 were primarily worked out between businessmen and organized labor. Often, as James Weinstein has shown in *The Corporate Ideal in the Liberal State, 1900–1918* (1968), it was businessmen who initially favored compensation plans (to protect themselves against the large payments which courts sometimes awarded in injury cases), and it was only with difficulty that they persuaded organized labor to go along. In practice, the benefits provided under the new laws were often not very generous and many types of workers were excluded. But the new system was better than the old one, and it laid the foundations for the disability provisions of the Social Security System.

The social progressives accomplished much. Their main contribution was to investigate and expose the worse abuses which workers suffered and to campaign for their amelioration. But progressives did not act alone in shaping the details of social legislation. Businessmen, labor unions, and party organizations commonly entered the fray when their own interests were at stake, and, in the bargaining which followed, the middle-class reformers' point of view frequently was submerged. When they prevailed, it often was because new-stock legislators from the urban party machines gave them crucial support, as John D. Buenker demonstrated in *Urban Liberalism and Progressive Reform*. New York State, for instance, adopted some fifty laws for factory safety and industrial welfare after the Triangle Shirtwaist Company fire of 1911 which killed 146 working women. This legislation was enacted chiefly through the action of the Tammany Hall Democratic machine and the legislative initiative of its leaders, Robert F. Wagner and Alfred E. Smith. In other instances, even the combined weight of the middle-class progressive organizations and the immigrant-backed party machines could not prevent proposed labor laws from being watered down or defeated.

Even when the desired reforms became law, the results often were ambiguous. Many reformers, and still more of their supporters among the general public, assumed that passing a law was equivalent to solving a problem and that government officials could be entrusted to enforce the measure in a progressive spirit. This frequently was not the case. Even progressives who were influenced by socialistic doctrines, as many were, worked within the existing political system and sometimes were defeated by it. In practice, at least, they accepted industrial capitalism and sought mainly to curtail its excesses. Unavoidably, too, the reformers' own cultural and class biases affected their actions. Yet, in spite of these limitations, they managed to better the lives of many industrial workers and to blunt class conflict. They were proud of these accomplishments.

Social progressives believed inevitably in social control as well as in social justice. Their view of justice was simplistic, traditional, and moralistic; for most of them it sprang from Christianity and the Social Gospel, for many from women's awareness of social injustice, and, for a significant minority, from Christian and secular socialism. To the social progressives, justice meant that all Americans should have an equal opportunity to live a decent life: that is, to be well fed and housed, to be clean, and to be moral human beings. Vague though these phrases were, most of the social progressives felt they had a fairly clear idea of what decent life meant, and that is where the element of social control entered their program. As middle-class Protestant Americans, they could not help but link injustice with deviations from what they considered to be right standards of behavior; nor could they prevent themselves from instinctively approving reforms which encouraged such behavior. Characteristically, that encouragement took the form of environmental changes rather than coercive restraints and was relatively benign compared to the control sought by some other progressives. Even so, it was control to some degree, and it implied a measure of repressiveness.

THE REFORMING PROFESSIONALS

Compared to the settlement-house kind of reformers whom we have called social progressives, the trained professionals whose reformism lay in the application of their special skills to social problems had a somewhat different conception of social justice and social control. Briefly, justice to them meant giving all elements of society the benefit of their expertise; control meant authorizing them to take whatever steps they thought necessary to achieve that justice. Those who successfully brought their skills to bear on recognized problems won considerable prestige for doing so. But there is no reason to doubt that the majority of them were sincere reformers. Many, if not most, shared the same Protestant evangelical fervor for good works which moved the social progressives. Almost all the trained professionals, moreover, were genuinely convinced that their methods offered the key to social harmony and justice.

There were not, at first, clear lines between the reforming professionals and the other social progressives. It would be hard to say at what point settlement-house residents became social workers, for example, but the organization of formal professional associations in this period provides the surest sign that this metamorphosis was occurring. Those who made the transition to scientific reform belonged to what Robert H. Wiebe has labeled the "new middle class" (*The Search for Order*). Confident, cosmopolitan, and educated, they earnestly desired "to remake the world upon their private models." Better than any previous historian, Wiebe has described their impulse to change their society. Quite properly, he has placed the social thought of the new middle class in the context of the important intellectual changes of this era, and he has made a sophisticated analysis of both their convictions and their uncertainties. But the result, in places, is an abstract, even mystical, account of what moved the reformers. For many of them, the reality must have been simpler than that: they believed they had scientific solutions to social problems and, out of altruism as well as professional ambition, wanted to apply them.

Few people living in the United States during the first decade of the twentieth century could doubt that medical doctors possessed a large fund of socially useful knowledge and skill. The germ theory of disease, now almost a generation old, had led bacteriologists to identify the specific microorganisms responsible for certain of the most feared diseases, particularly syphilis and tuberculosis. By 1909, an arsenical preparation, Salvarsan, had been proved effective against syphilis. Doctors seemed to be on the verge of eliminating bacterial infections. In surgery, significant advances had already been achieved through germ-killing procedures (antisepsis) and the use of germ-free operating environments (asepsis). The modern hospital, too, emerged in these years. From a charitable institution where poor patients went to die, the hospital by 1920 had become the primary center for the medical treatment of all social classes and the base for medical education. The training of doctors also became much more rigorous in the early 1900s. This was due in part to the influence of a major report on medical education in the United States, financed by the Carnegie Foundation and written by Abraham Flexner in 1910. But it was also due to the general drive of physicians to enhance their status by raising standards and eliminating quackery. The reorganization of the American Medical Association in 1901 and the surge in its membership from 8,400 to 70,000 during the following decade testified to the growing professionalization of doctors.

These advances inspired physicians to believe that, by playing consciously social roles, they could make enormous headway in preventing and curing disease. Their rising prestige correspondingly encouraged the public to entrust the doctors with significant authority. In consequence, progressive medical specialists, who worked through numerous voluntary health organizations, undertook successful crusades against such diseases as hookworm in the rural South and dysentery and cholera in the large cities. They campaigned to guarantee the availability of pure water for urban residents and pasteurized milk for infants. Perhaps most dramatically, they led public drives against tuberculosis and venereal disease.

The "white plague," as tuberculosis was called, struck particularly in the crowded tenement districts and seemed to single out the young as its chief victims. Men and women with the disease, labeled "lungers," were often socially ostracized for fear that they would infect others. This made tuberculosis almost a taboo subject of conversation, and few of the diseased would even admit to having it. Thus the first task of the anti-T.B. crusaders was the familiar progressive job of education. People had to be persuaded to receive treatment and to send others for treatment. The National Tuberculosis Association, founded in 1904 with medical men in the lead, educated doctors and laymen alike about the disease and persuaded local governments to support sanitaria (where victims of the disease were hospitalized), to pass antispitting ordinances, and to fund campaigns of education. T.B. mortality rates fell significantly in the years after 1900. Although improvements in living and housing standards probably had more to do with this than did the doctors' campaign, the physicians seem to have accelerated the decline of the disease, and, in any event, they provided a model which other progressive professionals followed.

Venereal disease also was a taboo subject. Most people recognized a connection between V.D. and prostitution. However, few persons knew how often syphilis was transmitted back to innocent wives, who in turn infected their unborn children, and even fewer talked about the subject in public. The social hygiene movement—as the doctors' assault on V.D. was called—thus became first a campaign of education to break what John C. Burnham has labeled "the conspiracy of silence" about sex and to support a drive to persuade those who were infected to accept treatment. ("The Progressive Era Revolution in American Attitudes toward Sex," *Journal of American History,* 1973). Led by Dr. Prince A. Morrow of New York, the social hygiene crusaders forged a natural alliance with the so-called "social-purity" forces whose main target was prostitution. Together, they broke the public's silence on sex, contributed significantly to getting syphilitics treated, and helped to curtail toleration of prostitution in the cities. "The physicians' campaign" for social hygiene, Burnham has written, "stands as a classic example of a progressive reform. Like other progressive reformers, Morrow and his group were inspired by moral fervor and sought to impose social change from above."

Psychiatry, too, went through a significant transformation in the progressive era, and its practitioners took on new social roles. In the late nineteenth century, the alienist (as the psychiatrist was then called) typically found himself isolated in a state asylum, where he kept custody of patients whom he did not know how to cure. His research, focused on the microscopic search for brain lesions which could be associated with specific behavioral symptoms, led nowhere. Then in the 1890s and early 1900s, a reorientation of the profession began. Led by Dr. Adolph Meyer of New York, psychiatrists increasingly associated mental disease with social and psychological, not merely physical, causes. The new psychiatrist, who worked in schools and prisons, collaborated with social workers and educated laymen, and became, in Barbara Sicherman's words, "a man of science with a social mission" ("The Quest for Mental Health in America, 1880–1917," see below, p. 136). To carry out that mission, Meyer—together with Clifford Beers, a crusading former mental patient—organized the National Committee for Mental Hygiene (NCMH) in 1909. Although somewhat vague in its goals, the NCMH encouraged the prevention and treatment of mental disease in its full social context and contributed yet another voice to the progressive demand for improving the environment.

Hopeful as it seemed, the mental hygiene movement never fulfilled its entire promise. Chronic and incurable patients remained confined to overcrowded asylums (now called hospitals) where, as David J. Rothman has written in *Conscience and Convenience: The Asylum and Its Alternatives in Progressive America* (1980), they commonly were ignored and often mistreated. Psychiatrists, for all their new insights into the social causes of mental disease, still had little knowledge about the cure of intractable cases. When the public's interest in mental hygiene waned, low governmental appropriations relegated the hospitals to the condition of backwater institutions. This was not the psychiatrists' fault (even now, little is known about the causes and cure of severe mental illnesses), but, like some other progressive professionals, their reach for new social roles somewhat exceeded their grasp.

Social workers literally tried to emulate the doctors. As Roy Lubove has shown in *The Professional Altruist: The Emergence of Social Work as a Career, 1880–1930* (1965), it was through association with physicians and psychiatrists that social workers gained some of their earliest footholds as professionals who utilized a distinctive skill to address a serious social problem. The skill was differential casework. As staff members in hospitals or psychiatric clinics, social workers began to develop methods to treat clients individually, each as a product of his or her own social and personal setting. This became the hallmark of the profession. Casework had its roots in the old practice of friendly "visiting" carried on by nineteenth-century charity volunteers who called on paupers. Now, with the environmental understanding of poverty taking hold, the old method was stripped of moralism and imbued with science. It depended on collecting and classifying data; it required specialized knowledge in psychology, mental testing, sociology, and medicine; and it called for professionals, not volunteers. Love of humanity was less useful than mastery of technique.

The development and refinement of the casework method met one of the most important social needs recognized by progressives even while it validated the social workers' standing as professionals. These purposes were not necessarily contradictory. The recognition that the social worker's skills were essential to the functioning of school systems, prisons, hospitals, and governmental agencies fulfilled an important progressive goal. But professionalism was not identical with reformism. The improvement of training, tightening of requirements, and creation of a "professional subculture" (in Lubove's words) tended to give methods the edge over zeal and function primacy over cause. In a sense, however, this transition actually fulfilled, rather than undermined, progressivism, for what had distinguished the reforming professionals all along was their drive for the systematic application of scientific techniques to social problems. This the social workers achieved.

So did progressive educators. For almost every social problem of the early twentieth century, somebody offered a solution which focused on the schools. In consequence, this was a time of remarkable educational innovation and experimentation. The kindergarten movement, begun in Germany and endorsed, as we have noted, by settlement workers, swept across the United States. By 1920, the kindergarten was firmly established as a major instrumentality of American education. The public high school, too, became a familiar institution which offered subjects ranging from vocational training to academic courses which now were attuned to college and university entrance requirements. In 1900, there were 6,000 high schools in the United States; twenty years later there were 14,000. All these innovations were based upon a new educational theory, expressed most fully by John Dewey of the University of Chicago and Columbia University. Education, he said, ought to begin with the student's own experience and should prepare the student to take charge of his or her own destiny in an industrial society. In practice, this prescription was broad enough to be interpreted freely—and it was, by professional educators with all sorts of progressive programs. Many of those programs involved the standardization of educational achievements and testing to see if the standards had been met.

The South was the center of the most dramatic progressive effort to improve educational standards. The Southern Education Board—an organization of northern philanthropists and southern educators and publicists—launched a crusade during the first decade of the twentieth century to improve the badly neglected public schools in the states of the old Confederacy. North Carolinians led the way by generating public enthusiasm for education, pumping large additional funds into schools, lengthening the school term, and increasing enrollments. Other states of the South followed suit. Against the wishes of at least some of the participating northern philanthropists, who traditionally had supported black education in the South, most of the region's crusade for literacy was focused on the white schools. By 1915, South Carolina (an extreme example) was spending twelve times as much per capita for the education of white children as it did for black children. As a result of these efforts, the illiteracy rate among southern whites was cut in half between 1900 and 1920. Despite all their obstacles, southern blacks made heroic progress, often through educational self-improvement. Black illiteracy declined from 45.5 per cent in 1900 to 23 per cent in 1920.

A somewhat different campaign for raising and standardizing the quality of schooling was undertaken in the large cities, where professional educators, often with business allies, conducted a successful drive to centralize school administration. The movement was often led by university presidents, such as Nicholas Murray Butler of Columbia in New York, Charles W. Eliot of Harvard in Boston, and William Rainey Harper of the University of Chicago. They aimed to wrest control of the schools from local district committees, which often were politicized, and to concentrate power in a central school board with authority to appoint expert educators to improve and run the schools. In the reformers' view, the central task facing large city schools—that of preparing an ethnically diverse population of children for roles in a world transformed by industry and technology—was too complex to be left to amateur educators, parents, and politicians. Many large cities reshaped the administration of their schools along the lines which the experts proposed, often, however, in the face of opposition from parents and teachers, whose influence over schools now declined.

The development and use of intelligence tests was a third application of educational expertise to social problems in the progressive era. In this instance, the problems were those associated with the feebleminded. In the early 1900s, over one hundred cities established special classes for children thought to have low intelligence. Of even more widespread concern were the high rates of delinquency, prostitution, crime, and pauperism believed to occur among the mentally handicapped. In order to identify and deal with those whose low intelligence inclined them to antisocial behavior, American psychologists (inspired by the pioneering work of the Frenchman, Alfred Binet) devised tests to provide "scientific" measurements of mental ability. There were enormous problems associated with this endeavor—writing reliable test questions, interpreting and classifying the results, and insuring that intelligence rather than education actually was being measured. As we know today, IQ tests were often used to confirm racial, class, and ethnic prejudices. Nevertheless they seemed to be valuable tools for social reformers. Psychologists, such as Henry H. Goddard of the Vineland Training School in New Jersey, subjected thousands of criminals and delinquents to their tests, and they found that an extremely high proportion of those who behaved antisocially were feebleminded. This discovery in turn led state legislators to provide for the institutionalization or even sterilization of the mentally defective. Between 1907 and 1917, sixteen states adopted legislation which authorized the sterilization of various categories of allegedly unfit individuals.

The menace of crime engaged the attention of an alliance of progressive experts which included lawyers, policemen, prison wardens, judges, and district attorneys. A key element of their program was the professionalization of police work, the least respected of the criminal justice occupations. This meant the separation of police departments from politics and the application of scientific methods to law enforcement and crime detection. Fingerprinting began to be commonly used after 1900. Police professionals also emulated other experts, especially social workers; for example, big-city departments began to hire policewomen to deal with juvenile and female offenders.

As this practice suggests, the progressives considered law breaking a social problem and believed that the individual criminal should be treated humanely. Programs for the rehabilitation of prisoners gained wide support, especially after some well-publicized experiments suggested that they could work. In the South, the brutal practice of leasing out convicts to private contractors was largely abolished, although the new state-use system was sometimes only marginally more humane. Probation, parole, and the indeterminate sentence—the most characteristic progressive innovations in the criminal justice field—epitomized the notion of treating each criminal as an individual. In practice, however, these programs proved difficult to administer. When public enthusiasm for criminal justice reform slackened and funds dwindled, probation and parole suffered badly. Nonetheless, the progressive experts had managed to introduce most of the major reforms which have dominated twentieth-century criminal justice.

City planners, too, applied their skills to the cure of social ills. Settlement workers, as we have seen, had grasped the need to reorganize urban neighborhoods, and, by 1909, when the National Conference on City Planning was organized, a core of professionals was developing a specialized body of techniques for that purpose. Zoning was their main tool, and hundreds of municipalities followed the planners' suggestions by enacting comprehensive zoning ordinances. But zoning had its limits. Just as housing experts had discovered that restrictive codes would not by themselves build good tenements, planners soon learned that zoning was more useful in preventing bad allocations of city space than in guaranteeing good ones. Still, their profession thrived and was encouraged by the growing number of universities which offered courses in city planning, the number of large cities which employed professionals to draw up comprehensive plans for revitalization, and the hundreds of counties and smaller towns which established planning boards and commissions. In 1917, the city planners signaled their permanence by creating their own professional association—the American City Planning Institute.

A final body of experts was concerned with the problems of country life. Educators, journalists, and businessmen constituted what William L. Bowers has called "an emerging professional rural leadership" who sought to stir public interest in farm life and to improve its quality (*The Country Life Movement in America, 1900-1920,* 1974). No farm problem was beyond the purview of the so-called country life movement: the difficulties of marketing crops, the decline of rural population, the scarcity of hired help, the rise of farm tenancy, the high cost of technological innovations, the poor quality of rural schools, and the loneliness and deprivation of country living. To address these ills, the leaders of the movement proposed characteristic progressive remedies, many of which were summarized in the report, in 1909, of the Commission on Country Life appointed by President Roosevelt the year before. Science and education not surprisingly were the movement's most important methods. Through carefully conducted surveys, country life advocates collected information on farmers and farm problems; by expanding educational extension work, they sought to spread knowledge of scientific farming; at rural life conferences, they exchanged information and aroused people to action. The movement's members also applied pressure for federal assistance to farmers, and several key acts passed during the Wilson and Harding administrations testify at least in part to their prodding. These federal measures helped farmers to solve their marketing problems, supported agricultural education, and, most important, expanded agricultural credit. But Bowers' study of the movement also reveals that farmers tended to resent the interference of the self-appointed, if well-intentioned, nonfarming professionals who claimed to have expert solutions for the ills of what they quaintly called country life.

The progressive professionals accomplished a great deal, but seldom as much as they hoped to do. Their goal was what Walter Lippmann called "mastery"—the use of scientific techniques to control the forces of social change and to shape the future (*Drift and Mastery,* 1914). The progressive professionals often made dramatic breakthroughs—against disease, for instance, and against illiteracy in the South. Even when their particular objects remained elusive, the reforming professionals won certification as the recognized experts in their fields.

There were many reasons why the experts did not always achieve their stated goals. Sometimes the methods of the professionals were simply unequal to the enormous tasks at hand. In many cases, the professionals were unable to win support from those persons whom they desired to assist or to maintain such support after the public's initial excitement had waned. Such a turnabout could be disastrous if the program in question was complex and required substantial governmental funding. Experiments in probation and parole, for example, succumbed in this manner. The reforming professionals frequently found themselves restrained by key business elites, such as the officers of philanthropic foundations. In *War and Welfare: Social Engineering in America, 1890-1925* (1980), John F. McClymer has shown how progressive "social engineers" were dependent on, and, in a sense, subservient to, the Russell Sage Foundation. A similar dependence bound many of the crusading physicians to the Rockefeller Foundation. Finally, the experts in almost every area experienced tensions between the allure of professionalism and the urge to pursue social reform.

These considerations suggest the need to qualify the notion that the "new middle class" was somehow supreme in the progressive era. The professionals were a confident and influential elite, but they were also beleaguered. They won formal recognition as experts, but they still remained under obligation to various masters, public and private.

What of the progressive professionals' ideas about social justice and social control? They tended to equate justice with the application of their expert methods, both because of the specific benefits conferred and because scientific techniques seemed inherently impartial. This was a relatively unexamined assumption—frequently an unstated one—but it curiously has prevailed to the present day, despite a good deal of contrary evidence. The progressive professionals frankly recognized the need for social control. By it they usually meant permitting the experts to compel compliance with their methods and to set standards of behavior and achievement in the areas of their competence. This could involve greater coerciveness than the controls sought by the social progressives, but the restrictions tended to be narrowly defined. No progressive trait has been more enduring than the tendency to entrust experts with social controls in the hope that they will achieve for us what Lippmann called "mastery" over the forces of change.

THE COERCIVE PROGRESSIVES

The third impulse from which progressive social reform sprang was the urge of many native-born Americans to impose their own ways of living upon other racial and ethnic groups. Racial and cultural intolerance was not, of course, the exclusive property of these reformers; many, perhaps most, Americans of the day shared it. Nor should it be assumed that all progressives approved the more coercive measures; on the contrary, these were the most controversial reforms of the age.

Such qualifications notwithstanding, the laws adopted to restrain ethnic minorities (and sometimes others, as well) bear considerable resemblance to the less coercive progressive social reforms. The gathering of social data, the influence of science, the use of moralistic rhetoric, and the reliance on the hand of government all were present here, just as they were in the more benign progressive crusades. What distinguished the coercive, intolerant reforms from the others was not their methods, or even the type of appeals on which they were based, so much as the distinctive balance which they struck (or often failed to strike) between the familiar goals of social justice and social control. Justice is difficult to find in some of these reforms, at least to judge from the intentions of their supporters and the results which they achieved. Instead, these measures reflected a preponderant devotion to social control.

No group fared worse at the hands of their fellow Americans during the progressive era than did the blacks, who were effectively disfranchised and socially segregated between 1890 and 1910. As C. Vann Woodward has shown in *The Strange Career of Jim Crow* (3rd rev. ed., 1974), southern race relations remained in flux during the final decades of the nineteenth century. Some institutions (such as schools) were almost thoroughly segregated, while others (such as transportation facilities) often were not. Blacks occupied a subordinate position, to be sure, but conditions had not yet crystalized into the rigid, brutal racial repression that came to characterize the twentieth-century South.

Several developments brought about the transition to the new system of disfranchisement and segregation toward the end of the 1800s. One was the increasing disposition of northern whites to discontinue the federal government's historic efforts to protect southern blacks. A series of Supreme Court decisions, which in effect accepted racial discrimination, reflected this trend. During the same period, the nation's new imperialistic ventures into the nonwhite lands of the world convinced many Americans that colored peoples were not fit for self-government and spurred their willingness to let southern whites handle domestic race relations in their own ways. Further buttressing this change of attitude was the rise of purportedly scientific theories of white, or "Aryan," superiority. These theories, drawn from the new social science of anthropology, classified peoples into hereditary categories, arranged in order of merit. Northern European Caucasians were located at the top of the scale, while Negroes were at or near the bottom.

Developments within the South also served to encourage the more virulent racial repressiveness of the early twentieth century. The defeat of the Populists (many of whom had tried to bring about cooperation between poor farmers of both races) led to widespread agreement among whites that blacks must never again hold the balance of power in the South. Indeed, according to the new white orthodoxy, blacks had to be further submerged in order to make way for the advancement of the superior race. Voicing this violent pronouncement was a new breed of southern politician, skilled at harking back to the demands of the Populists (without endorsing Populism's more radical proposals) and equally adept at issuing the most extreme demands for white supremacy. Thus the stage was set for the reign of Jim Crow.

Beginning around 1900, states and cities throughout the South enacted a flood of laws which brought about the nearly complete separation of black and white life. Segregation on railroad cars and streetcars was legally mandated by every southern state during the first years of the new century. "White only" and "Colored only" signs appeared on water fountains, toilets, theater entrances, and restaurants. Recreation facilities, too, were segregated, including ball fields, motion-picture houses, and parks. State and local institutions, such as hospitals, asylums, and jails, also were segregated by race. No detail was too minute to be placed on the statute books, even down to a provision for separate Bibles on which black and white witnesses could take their oaths in court. The racial segregation which had been practiced haphazardly in the decades after Reconstruction now became completely compelled by law.

In what sense were the Jim Crow laws progressive? Not at all was the traditional answer of early historians of progressivism who identified themselves with the cause of social reform. The true progressive spirit in race relations, they said, was embodied in those reformers, both black and white, who founded the National Association for the Advancement of Colored People (NAACP) in 1909. This organization, so characteristically progressive in its methods, appealed to the nation's conscience for a cessation of the violence against blacks (especially lynching) and for the establishment of social and political equality. Even historians sympathetic to progressivism had to admit, however, that the racially egalitarian work of the NAACP drew only a miniscule number of supporters. Most progressives, according to this interpretation, simply had a "blind spot" in regard to race relations. The reformers' overall failure to give sympathetic attention to the plight of black Americans thus represented an anomaly, a deviation from the essence of progressivism.

This viewpoint ignores the intimate relationship between racism and progressivism in the South. As Woodward has observed, "the typical progressive reformer rode to power in the

South on a disfranchising or white-supremacy movement" (*The Strange Career of Jim Crow*). Jack Temple Kirby has carried the point even further: "The great race settlement of 1890–1910—black disfranchisement and segregation—was itself the seminal 'progressive' reform of the era" (*Darkness at the Dawning: Race and Reform in the Progressive South,* 1972). Whether the repression of blacks was the "seminal" reform in the South, or just one of many, it was unquestionably tied to the post-Populist reconciliation among southern whites, without which the struggles to reform and improve life among white people would not have gone forward. The traditional historical interpretation also neglects the general progressive tendency toward social control, of which Jim Crow was but an extreme expression. For beyond the South, too, the impulse to restrain and repress particular elements in the population, especially immigrants, was one aspect of progressivism.

The implications of progressivism for immigrant life were exceedingly complex. As numerous historians have observed, the reformers often identified various social and political evils with foreign-born Americans. Intemperance, immorality, illiteracy, and corruption all seemed to flourish in the swollen immigrant ghettoes of the large cities. Correspondingly, the foreign born frequently took a dim view of the progressives. In Richard Hofstadter's words: "The reformer was a mystery. Often he stood for things that to the immigrant were altogether bizarre, like women's rights and Sunday [blue] laws, or downright insulting, like temperance. His abstractions had no appeal within the immigrant experience—citizenship, responsibility, efficiency, good government, economy, businesslike management" (*The Age of Reform*). Not surprisingly, then, progressives and immigrants often treated each other as enemies.

Perhaps as often, however, they were mutually supportive. As we have noted earlier, immigrants and their political representatives frequently provided essential support for social welfare and labor reforms. Not every progressive, moreover, regarded the immigrant as an enemy. In his brilliant study of

American attitudes toward the foreign born, *Strangers in the Land: Patterns of American Nativism, 1860–1925* (1955), John Higham emphasized the optimistic, tolerant side of progressivism. He labeled it "a movement that had little need of nativism." The activities of many of the settlement-house progressives support Higham's judgment. Settlement workers commonly devoted a great deal of energy to encouraging and perpetuating the distinctive cultures brought to the United States by the newcomers. Jane Addams' poignant essay, "Immigrants and Their Children" (*Twenty Years at Hull-House*, 1910), describes how settlement workers in Chicago taught second-generation immigrants to be proud of their parents' old-world ways and values. These were the "gifts" which immigrants brought to America.

Even Higham had to admit, however, that the progressives could talk in generalities about immigrant gifts far more easily than they could define them. "When examples of specific gifts came to mind, they turned out invariably to be things to which Americans attached slight importance: folk dances, music, exotic dishes, handicrafts, perhaps certain literary fragments." Jane Addams' essay closes on a note which similarly suggests the progressives' restricted conception of what was valuable in immigrant life: she hoped that it would not be impossible to promote "American citizenship" and, at the same time, to preserve older cultural ways and values. Behind even the most tolerant rhetoric lay the reformers' concern to encourage certain uniform habits and beliefs among the immigrants. The word "Americanization" came into use to describe the progressive programs to persuade immigrants to adopt the ways of their new homeland.

Education was a principal vehicle of Americanization. Public and parochial schools, as well as business corporations, sought to hurry the process of assimilating the immigrants by giving them instruction in American values. "I am an American" was the first sentence taught in the Ford Motor Company's English-language classes. Patriotic societies, such as the Daughters of the American Revolution and the Society of

Colonial Dames, joined the crusade for Americanization by presenting patriotic lectures, distributing pamphlets, and sponsoring civics classes. Chambers of commerce, labor unions, and churches, too, participated in these projects, whose goal was to inculcate the rejection of alien habits and a submission to the "spirit of true Americanism." Much of this propaganda was helpful to the immigrant who wanted to get ahead in the United States, and some of it was harmless. But certain features of the crusade for Americanization were downright coercive, especially during the later progressive years when the World War made many Americans more fearful of all things alien.

The most important expression of that fear was the demand for sharp restrictions on immigration to the United States. The movement for restriction began in the 1880s with the exclusion of the Chinese (who were detested in California) and of certain allegedly undesirable classes of men and women, including paupers, prostitutes, and anarchists. The labor violence of the 1880s and the economic depression of the succeeding decade evoked further demands to limit immigration, especially from the nations of southern and eastern Europe, whose peoples were widely presumed to be least fit for American citizenship. With the return of prosperity as the nineteenth century ended, the clamor for restriction waned. By the time that the exclusionist movement had regained strength about a decade later, its nativist proponents had learned to utilize progressive methods— investigation, education, and legislation.

The exclusionists formed societies to expound the benefits of restriction, gathered data which demonstrated the evils of unlimited immigration, and pressured governmental officials to take action. In 1907, Congress turned down the restrictionists' demand for a literacy test for admission to the United States but created a commission to study every aspect of the immigration problem. The commission's voluminous report, issued four years later, said that unlimited immigration created unmanageable social problems and endorsed a literacy test. To the applause of many social progressives, Presidents Taft and Wilson vetoed such a requirement in 1913, 1915, and 1917, but it became law over Wilson's veto in the latter year. This measure represented the exclusionists' first great victory. Helped by the World War and by the intolerance which followed, truly exclusionist quotas on immigration became law in 1921 and 1924 and thus ended one of the greatest folk migrations of all time. Many reformers were appalled by the virtual ban on immigration, but no one could deny that restriction had been accomplished through characteristic progressive methods and with the aid of progressive appeals.

The alleged propensity of immigrants to drink too much particularly worried reformers. The social life of immigrant men in the cities often centered in the saloon, an institution which progressives regarded as inimical to harmonious family life, health, and hard work. Many native-born Americans were intemperate, too, with the same ill effects on what the reformers considered to be decent life. More completely than any other crusade of the era, the prohibition of alcoholic beverages illustrates how many progressives sincerely supported social controls for moral, scientific, and economic reasons.

The puritanical moralizing and social intolerance of the prohibition movement should not obscure the seriousness of the evils to which temperance advocates were responding. For a full century, from the early 1820s until the adoption of national prohibition one hundred years later, American reformers from almost every background crusaded against the menace of drink. Late in the 1800s, that menace seemed to become more threatening than ever. Investments in the liquor business soared, saloons multiplied, and drunkenness appeared to increase everywhere, especially in the cities. By the early 1900s, there was abundant scientific evidence which linked alcohol to insanity, cirrhosis, heart disease, and numerous other serious illnesses. Social workers observed the connections between drink and prostitution, the deterioration of family life, and unemployment. Businessmen decried the toll taken by alcohol upon the efficiency and the reliability, not to mention the safety, of industrial workers. Political reformers recognized that the liquor industry had become a potent source of corruption.

Many of the temperance reformers no doubt exaggerated these evils. Certainly, too, they mixed in a great deal of cultural intolerance and economic greed with genuine scientific and humanitarian concerns. But such a mixture of motives only serves to emphasize how characteristic of progressive social reform the crusade against alcohol was. No organization exhibits this better than the Anti-Saloon League (ASL), which was founded in 1895 and became one of the most effective agencies of political pressure and moral suasion in American history. The ASL worked closely with the Protestant churches and concentrated at first on measures of local option or statewide prohibition. By 1917, the ASL was so successful that three fourths of the American people lived in dry counties, while two thirds of the states had adopted prohibition.

By the eve of American entry into the war, the ASL had begun to campaign for a national prohibition amendment, with real prospects for success. The war brought the reformers even closer to victory, as ASL spokesmen succeeded in identifying prohibition with patriotism, in forbidding the sale of alcoholic beverages near military bases, and in getting the nation to conserve badly needed grain by drastically reducing the alcoholic content of beer. Late in 1917, Congress passed and submitted to the states the Eighteenth Amendment which would prohibit the manufacture, sale, or transportation of alcoholic beverages in the United States. Many progressives hailed the amendment, which went into effect in 1920, as the greatest triumph for morality since the abolition of slavery. The record of evasion and corrupt enforcement which followed during the 1920s ought not to blind us to the sincerity of the prohibitionists' belief.

The coercive progressive social movements placed a greater emphasis on social control than did the reforms advocated by the settlement-house workers and progressive professionals. But the same basic drive for control motivated nearly every movement for social reform of the progressive era. Progressives sincerely believed that justice depended on such control. We can lament the fact that in practice justice often took second place to social control, but we must, at the same time, appreciate the reformers' conviction that the two were entwined and inseparable.

That the urge to impose social control often overshadowed the desire for social justice is another example of the distinction between the rhetoric, intentions, and results of progressivism. In their language and appeals, the reformers commonly gave greater weight to justice than to coercion, while in their actual methods they tended to rely on controls. The progressives often failed to recognize the degree to which the aim of justice could be neglected in the actual administration of a reform. Often, as well, the means which the progressives used simply failed to achieve what had been expected of them. Today we are far more conscious of the limitations of progressive techniques than were the reformers of the early twentieth century. It is significant, however, that while the progressives' methods of trying to bring justice and order to an industrial society have been criticized, even repudiated, they have not been replaced by fundamentally different means of social reform.

FOUR

Epilogue: The Decline and Endurance of Progressivism

Wilson's call for American entry into the World War in April 1917 created a crisis of conscience for most progressives. Besides hating the barbaric war for its own sake, reformers feared that participation in the conflict would divert attention from economic and social problems at home. Many progressives, moreover, believed that bankers and industrialists had caused American involvement in order to protect their loans to the Allied nations, especially Great Britain. As late as the eve of American entry into the war, Wilson himself had given strong expression to the conviction that war and progressivism were antithetical. "Every reform we have won," he declared, "will be lost if we go into this war."

But once forced into war, Wilson proved brilliantly adept in fashioning a progressive rationale for America's participation on the Allied side. The war, he said, would be a war to make the world safe for democracy, to protect the rights of small nations, and to end militarism and navalism. Wilson deeply believed that these goals were possible, and never was he more articulate or moving than when he expressed his war aims in 1917 and 1918. Many Socialists and most progressives were converted to the President's point of view; indeed, they realized that the war provided an opportunity for extensive reform at home and the achievement of a liberal international postwar order. John Dewey saw such "social possibilities" in the war as "the more conscious and extensive use of science for communal purposes." Walter Lippmann declared: "Out of this horror ideas have arisen to possess men's souls. . . . We can dare to hope for things which we never dared to hope for in the past."

Not every reformer saw such hopeful opportunities. Randolph Bourne, a pacifist intellectual, vehemently denied that a murderous international conflict could promote progressive goals of any sort. He reminded reformers of their earlier opposition to the war and pointedly asked them: "If the war is too strong for you to prevent, how is it going to be weak enough for you to control and mould to your liberal purposes?" The question was incisive and unanswerable. Many progressives later sorrowfully concluded that Bourne had been right. In 1917, however, most of them welcomed the possibilities which war seemed to offer to make the nation more progressive and to free the world from the menace of militarism.

To mobilize Americans and their resources for a total war

required considerable feats of persuasion and organization. Not surprisingly, many wartime endeavors bore a striking resemblance to progressive crusades. To get each person to do his or her part—whether as a soldier, an employer, a laborer, or simply as a loyal citizen—required intervention to an extreme degree. This was achieved in many instances through voluntary methods, but, when necessary, through governmental coercion. However it occurred, the war effort was organized along bureaucratic lines. In particular, this meant close governmental supervision of the nation's productive resources. Above all, the war effort depended on vigorous, carefully designed appeals to the new public opinion of the progressive era. And the basic message of those appeals was that the war was a great moral undertaking.

No wartime task was carried out in a more progressive manner than that of raising and training an American army to relieve the beleaguered Allied forces in the trenches on the western fronts of Europe. The Selective Service Act, adopted in the spring of 1917, made all young men eligible for the draft and established a governmental bureaucracy to register and choose them. Amidst the coercion, however, there remained—as David M. Kennedy has observed—a significant aura of voluntarism about the draft, expressed by the word "service" and exemplified by local civilian administration (*Over Here: The First World War and American Society,* 1980). Once enlisted, the nation's soldiers were subjected to a nearly complete battery of social controls. Kept from alcohol, warned against prostitutes, inspected for disease, tested for intelligence, and ministered to by the Red Cross, the YMCA, and army chaplains, the army was rendered as morally and scientifically "fit to fight" as the wisest and most religious progressives of the day could make it.

Scientific learning, bureaucratic organization, and a mixture of voluntarism with coercion were also put to use to mobilize industry and agriculture. A War Industries Board allocated raw materials, controlled production, and supervised labor relations in an extraordinary harnessing of the American industrial machine to the war effort. A Food Administration under

Herbert Hoover achieved remarkable conservation in the consumption of food at home and, equally important, saw to the distribution of adequate food supplies to the armies and citizens of the Allied nations. To achieve these results, Hoover relied not only on planning but also upon persuasion. By appealing to American pride and patriotism, he persuaded farmers to grow more food and citizens to endure meatless and breadless days. Similar wartime accomplishments were achieved by the Fuel Administration and the Railroad Administration.

Most Americans were persuaded to support the war and to accept its coercions by a gigantic propaganda campaign conducted by the Committee on Public Information, which was established by the national government soon after the United States declared war. Headed by George Creel, a former muckraking journalist, the Committee on Public Information instituted a program of voluntary press censorship and then went on to mobilize lecturers, writers, artists, actors, and scholars to portray American war aims in idealistic terms and to characterize German militarism as the epitome of evil. Creel's propaganda, and, even more, that of voluntary organizations such as the National Security League, aroused an outbreak of war fervor such as the country had never before experienced. Public opinion was thus stimulated more powerfully on behalf of military action than reformers or independent politicians had ever aroused it on behalf of change during peacetime.

Compared to the European belligerents, all of which suppressed dissent and disloyalty in a draconian fashion, the United States Government, under authority of the Espionage Act of 1917 and the Sedition Act of 1918, dealt with opponents of the war with considerable restraint. There were 2,000 indictments under the Espionage and Sedition Acts and only 1,000 convictions—evidence that a measure of due process survived even during wartime. But it was not so with a large number of private groups and local and state bodies, particularly the state committees of public safety, many of which were in fact vigilante groups. Persons suspected of not supporting the war effort were sometimes beaten and tarred and feathered, and at least two were murdered. All this was done with a zeal more intense than—but not otherwise fundamentally different from—the passions which had infused some of the more coercive social reforms of the progressive era.

Like those reforms, the popular crackdown on wartime dissent had strong cultural and ethnic overtones. Much of the hysteria was focused on German Americans and all things associated with their homeland. Many states forbade the teaching of the German language in public schools and even outlawed church services conducted in that language. The hysteria was directed, as well, against other central European peoples and fostered a popular cry for "100 percent Americanism." Because of the war, immigration to the United States came to a virtual halt, but the nativist emotions generated during the conflict guaranteed that the coming of peace would be accompanied by renewed efforts to stop the influx of people from abroad. As we have seen, the movement to prohibit the consumption of alcoholic beverages also triumphed during the war, spurred to some degree by the association of drink with foreign peoples and their cultures.

Wartime repression and social conflict gave way to even greater outbreaks of fear and violence during 1919, the year of the Great Red Scare. The Bolshevik Revolution in Russia and the ensuing spread of Communism across Europe set off a wave of hysteria in the United States. Socialists, unionized workers, and genuine Communists were all lumped together in the tortured public mind. Many persons were arrested, and 556 alien Communists were ultimately deported. Such panic was to some degree a reflection of the disillusionment of Americans with the results of the war. A crusade to make the world safe for democracy had, it seemed, unleashed the Russian Reds, while the one great goal which most progressives could support—American membership in Wilson's League of Nations—fell victim to personal and partisan rivalries. Moreover, a rash of strikes and labor violence, fierce clashes between blacks and whites, and a soaring inflation in 1919 seemed once again to threaten the very fabric of American society.

Progressivism was both a perpetrator and a victim of this transition in the public mood. With the entry of the United States into the war, the moral fervor and confident interventionism which had distinguished early twentieth-century reform were fairly easily channeled into military actions against a foreign foe. And when those battles, although literally won in the field, began to appear not to have accomplished the more idealistic aims articulated by Wilson, it was again relatively easy to turn the passions born of progressivism against fellow Americans who allegedly were responsible for the failure of the Great Crusade to achieve its larger purposes. Persons different from Americans of the progressive era might not have been so disillusioned with the war. It ended, after all, in a complete military victory. But years of reform had inculcated a widespread tendency toward the use of overblown rhetoric and, worse still, the habit of believing it. Progressive Americans wanted to hear the war's purposes proclaimed in the loftiest terms, and, when those high goals inevitably failed to be achieved, enormous disappointment ensued.

The optimism that had inspired the kind of reforms which had flourished before 1917 was severely shaken. Some progressive reforms still remained popular, particularly the repressive ones, but many fell into disfavor, especially the more generous, altruistic reforms. Support for these had depended on a spirit of hopefulness. To be sure, progressive crusades had always met a mixed reception from Americans. But, after the war, the balance tipped against organized, ameliorative reform. A progressive movement which had been merely divided now became embattled.

The decline of the progressive spirit was signaled by intellectual developments which challenged the synthesis of thought and belief upon which early twentieth-century reform had rested. Henry F. May has shown that, for most of the progressive era, the basic doctrines of nineteenth-century American culture still remained intact: "The certainty and universality of moral values . . . [and] the inevitability, particularly in America, of progress" (*The End of American*

Innocence: A Study of the First Years of Our Own Time, 1912–1917, 1959). Just before and during the war, a small number of brilliant young American intellectuals refined—and even repudiated—the old doctrines. Some, like Walter Lippmann and Lincoln Steffens, had ties to socialism and progressivism; others were further outside the political mainstream; many were artists and writers. What they shared and expressed was a deep skepticism of familiar moral certitudes and of the supreme confidence of the bearers of the old culture. These intellectuals were celebrated figures in prewar America, and their numbers grew mightily in the 1920s. That some of the decade's brightest young men and women should reject, rather than accept, the optimistic tenets of reform was a telling blow to progressivism.

Progressivism waned after 1917, not primarily because of the war, but more because of the revival of profound social divisions and a growing intellectual malaise with reform. Nowhere was this waning more visible than on the political front. The "Bull Moose" party of 1912, which actually had been only Theodore Roosevelt's wing of the Republican party, had virtually collapsed by 1916, and conservatives were in unchallenged control of the national GOP. Moreover, by 1920, the Democratic progressive coalition was wrecked, a victim of disagreement over the League of Nations, of sectional and class disharmony among its members, and, not least, of political blunders. For a few years, progressivism had seemed capable of uniting reformers into a majority political coalition under the aegis of the Democratic party. In retrospect, it is clear that progressives always had been too diverse to remain united in a cohesive national political organization. After 1918, their inability to maintain such a coalition became obvious.

Divided, demoralized, and disorganized, progressivism nonetheless remained alive. Its persistence in various forms into the 1920s and beyond suggests that the spirit of reform still burned strongly and passionately among many Americans. To be sure, the reform temper no longer infused the broad reaches of American society as it had done during the previous two decades. Many middle-class Americans, in particular, had left the ranks of active reformers. The defectors included professionals contented with their new status, small businessmen who enjoyed the relative prosperity of the 1920s, and urban Americans who found satisfaction in what Arthur S. Link has termed "a whole new set of business values—mass production and consumption, short hours and high wages, full employment, welfare capitalism" ("What Happened to the Progressive Movement in the 1920s?" *American Historical Review,* 1959). Thus in the 1920s, to a far greater degree than in the heyday of progressivism, reform depended for its support upon farmers, industrial workers, and diverse, discontented minorities. These groups refused to let progressivism die.

In Congress, the so-called Farm Bloc advanced and enacted a program of relief for farmers which built upon the reforms adopted during the Wilson administration. Stockyards and packing houses came under strict federal regulation; farm cooperatives were exempted from the antitrust laws; and an entirely new system of rural credits was adopted. Of most importance to farmers, the concept of "parity"—the use of federal authority to obtain what farmers said were fair prices for their products—was persuasively advanced. Although presidential vetoes defeated "parity" for farmers in the 1920s, the concept gained such widespread support that it became enshrined in national policy during the era of the New Deal. The triumph of such a program suggested how deeply rooted was the progressive belief that government bore a special responsibility to protect depressed classes.

Other progressive endeavors also went forward during the 1920s, although they were commonly the products of special-interest group activity, not of a broad consensus. Conservation, the public development of natural resources, tariff reform, and immigration restriction were but four such progressive causes which continued to be successfully agitated. The continuation of reform in various cities and states across the country also testified to the endurance of progressivism. Indeed, it might be said that progressivism shifted from the federal to the state and local levels during the 1920s. While federal expenditures remained fairly constant during the decade, expenditures by state and local governments on schools, highways, and social services grew by an astounding 400 per cent from 1913 to 1932. Between these dates, state and local expenditures for education increased from $577 million to nearly $2.3 billion; for public welfare, from $52 million to $444 million; and for highways, from $419 million to $1.74 billion. The emergence and triumph of the New Deal in the 1930s showed that the reform tradition of the early twentieth century was still very much alive.

Alive, but it was no longer alive with the same special characteristics which had marked progressivism during the early 1900s, when it dominated public life in the United States. The ambivalence about the consequences of industrialism continued to pervade reform, although after 1920 there was never any serious challenge to the corporation as the basic economic institution of American society. Progressivism had contained at least the potential for such a challenge. Environmental interventionism, based on science, remained the most respected approach to reform, but it no longer enjoyed the heady confidence which the progressives had placed in its methods. This decline of optimism, and of the evangelical fervor which had accompanied it, constituted the most visible losses for the reform tradition. Americans would continue from time to time to try to improve their politics and society, but not with the same hopeful faith which they had possessed during the years from 1905 to 1917. While much of progressivism endured, the progressive era thus was over.

In this analysis we have frequently pointed to the differences between the rhetoric, intentions, and results of progressive reform. The failure of reform always to fulfill the expectations of its advocates was not, of course, unique to the progressive era. Jacksonian reform, Reconstruction, and the New Deal all exhibited similar ironies and disappointments. In each case, the clash between reformers with divergent purposes, the inability to predict how given methods of reform would work in practice, and the ultimate waning of popular zeal for change all contributed to the disjuncture of rationale, purpose, and achievement. Yet the gap between these things seems more obvious in the progressive era because so many diverse movements for reform took place in a brief span of time and were accompanied by resounding rhetoric and by high expectations for the improvement of the American social and political environment. The effort to change so many things all at once, and the grandiose claims made for the moral and material betterment which would result, meant that disappointments were bound to occur.

Yet even the great number of reforms and the uncommonly high expectations for them cannot fully account for the consistent gaps which we have observed between the stated purposes, real intentions, and actual results of progressivism. Several additional factors, intrinsic to the nature of early twentieth-century reform, help to explain the ironies and contradictions.

One of these was the progressives' confident reliance on modern methods of reform. Heirs of recent advances in natural science and social science, they enthusiastically devised and applied new techniques to improve American government and society. Their methods often worked; on the other hand, progressive programs often simply did not prove capable of accomplishing what had been expected of them. This was not necessarily the reformers' fault. They hopefully used untried methods even while they lacked a science of society which was capable of solving all the great problems which they attacked. At the same time, the progressives' scientific methods made it possible to know just how far short of success their programs had sometimes fallen. The evidence of their failures thus was more visible than in any previous era of reform. To the progressives' credit, they usually published that evidence—for contemporaries and historians alike to see.

A second aspect of early twentieth-century reform which helps to account for the gaps between aims and achievements was the deep ambivalence of the progressives about industrialism and its consequences. Individual reformers were divided, and so was their movement as a whole. Compared to many Americans of the late 1800s, the progressives fundamentally accepted an industrial society and sought mainly to control and ameliorate it. Even reformers who were intellectually committed to socialist ideas often acted the part of reformers, not radicals.

Yet progressivism was infused and vitalized, as we have seen, by people truly angry with their industrial society. Few of them wanted to tear down the modern institutions of business and commerce, but their anger was real, their moralism was genuine, and their passions were essential to the reforms of their time.

The reform movement never resolved this ambivalence about industrialism. Much of its rhetoric and popular passion pointed in one direction—toward some form of social democracy—while its leaders and their programs went in another. Often the result was confusion and bitterness. Reforms frequently did not measure up to popular, antibusiness expectations, indeed, never were expected to do so by those who designed and implemented them. Even conservative, ameliorative reformers like Theodore Roosevelt often used radical rhetoric. In doing so, they misled their followers and contributed to the ironies of progressivism.

Perhaps most significant, progressives failed to achieve all their goals because, despite their efforts, they never fully came to terms with the divisions and conflicts in American society. Again and again, they acknowledged the existence of social disharmony more fully and frankly than had nineteenth-century Americans. Nearly every social and economic reform of the era was predicated on the progressive recognition that diverse cultural and occupational groups had conflicting interests, and that the responsibility for mitigating and adjusting those differences lay with the whole society, usually the government. Such recognition was one of the progressives' most significant achievements. Indeed, it stands among the most important accomplishments of liberal reform in all of American history. For, by frankly acknowledging the existence of social disharmony, the progressives committed the twentieth-century United States to recognizing—and to lessening—the inevitable conflicts of a heterogeneous industrial society.

Yet the significance of the progressives' recognition of diversity was compromised by the methods and institutions which they adopted to diminish or eliminate social and economic conflict. Expert administrative government turned out to be less neutral than the progressives believed that it would be. No scientific reform could be any more impartial than the experts who gathered the data or than the bureaucrats who implemented the programs. In practice, as we have seen, administrative government often succumbed to the domination of special interests.

It would be pointless to blame the progressives for the failure of their new methods and programs to eradicate all the conflicts of an industrial society, but it is perhaps fair to ask why the progressives adopted measures which tended to disguise and obscure economic and social conflict almost as soon as they had uncovered it. For one thing, they honestly believed in the almost unlimited potentialities of science and administration. Our late twentieth-century skepticism of these wonders should not blind us to the faith with which the progressives embraced them and imbued them with what now seem magical properties. For another, the progressives were reformers, not radicals. It was one thing to recognize the existence of economic and social conflict, but quite another thing to admit that it was permanent. By and large, these men and women were personally and ideologically inclined to believe that the American society was, in the final analysis, harmonious, and that such conflicts as did exist could be resolved. Finally, the class and cultural backgrounds of the leading progressives often made them insensitive to lower-class immigrant Americans and their cultures. Attempts to reduce divisions sometimes came down to imposing middle-class Protestant ways on the urban masses. In consequence, the progressives never fulfilled their hope of eliminating social conflict. Reformers of the early twentieth century saw the problem more fully than had their predecessors, but they nonetheless tended to consider conflicts resolved when, in fact, they only had been papered over. Later twentieth-century Americans have also frequently deceived themselves in this way.

Thus progressivism inevitably fell short of its rhetoric and intentions. Lest this seem an unfairly critical evaluation, it is important to recall how terribly ambitious were the stated aims and true goals of the reformers. They missed some of their marks because they sought to do so much. And, despite all their shortcomings, they accomplished an enormous part of what they set out to achieve.

Progressivism brought major innovations to almost every facet of public and private life in the United States. The political and governmental systems particularly felt the effects of reform. Indeed, the nature of political participation and the uses to which it was put went through transitions as momentous as those of any era in American history. These developments were complex, as we have seen, and it is no easy matter to sort out who was helped and who was hurt by each of them or by the entire body of reforms. At the very least, the political changes of the progressive era significantly accommodated American public life to an urban-industrial society. On balance, the polity probably emerged neither more nor less democratic than before, but it did become better suited to address, or at least recognize, the questions and problems which arose from the cities and factories of the nation. After the progressive era, just as before, wealthier elements in American society had a disproportionate share of political power, but we can hardly conclude that this was the fault of the progressives.

The personal and social life of the American people was also deeply affected by progressivism. Like the era's political changes, the economic and social reforms of the early twentieth century were enormously complicated and are difficult to summarize without doing violence to their diversity. In the broadest sense, the progressives sought to mitigate the injustice and the disorder of a society now dominated by its industries and cities. Usually, as we have observed, the quests for social justice and social control were inextricably bound together in the reformers' programs, with each group of progressives having different interpretations of these dual ends. Justice sometimes took second place to control. However, before one judges the reformers too harshly for that, it is well to remember how bad urban social conditions were in the late nineteenth century and the odds against which the reformers fought. It is also well to remember that they often succeeded in mitigating the harshness of urban-industrial life.

The problems with which the progressives struggled have, by and large, continued to challenge Americans ever since. And, although the assumptions and techniques of progressivism no longer command the confidence which early twentieth-century Americans had in them, no equally comprehensive body of reforms has ever been adopted in their place. Throughout this study, we have criticized the progressives for having too much faith in their untried methods. Yet if this was a failing, it was also a source of strength, one now missing from reform in America. For the essence of progressivism lay in the hopefulness and optimism which the reformers brought to the tasks of applying science and administration to the high moral purposes in which they believed. The historical record of their aims and achievements leaves no doubt that there were many men and women in the United States in the early 1900s who were not afraid to confront the problems of a modern industrial society with vigor, imagination, and hope. They of course failed to solve all those problems, but no other generation of Americans has done conspicuously better in addressing the political, economic, and social conditions which it faced.

Bibliographical Essay

Few subjects in the history of the United States have attracted more attention from historians than early twentieth-century reform. The literature on progressivism is accordingly enormous. For a sense of how much historical work there has been, and for detailed bibliographies on particular aspects of the subject, the first place to turn is William M. Leary, Jr., and Arthur S. Link, comps., *The Progressive Era and the Great War, 1896–1920,* 2nd edn. (Arlington Heights, Ill., 1978). The student who feels in need of a comprehensive general history of the progressive era should read Arthur S. Link and William B. Catton, *American Epoch: A History of the United States Since 1900,* 2 vols., 5th edn. (New York, 1980).

Several scholars have undertaken the herculean task of surveying and evaluating the diverse recent writings on progressivism. Three such historiographical efforts, which proved valuable in writing the first chapter of this book, particularly deserve to be consulted: Robert H. Wiebe, "The Progressive Years, 1900-1917," in William H. Cartwright and Richard L. Watson, Jr., eds., *The Reinterpretation of American History and Culture* (Washington, D.C., 1973), pp.425-42; David M. Kennedy, "Overview: The Progressive Era," *Historian* 37 (1975): 453-68; and William G. Anderson, "Progressivism: An Historiographical Essay," *History Teacher* 5 (1973): 427-52. Four longer works provide successful interpretive syntheses of progressivism and its age: Otis L. Graham, Jr., *The Great Campaigns: Reform and War in America, 1900-1928* (Englewood Cliffs, N.J., 1971); William L. O'Neill, *The Progressive Years: America Comes of Age* (New York, 1975); Irwin Unger and Debi Unger, *The Vulnerable Years: The United States, 1896-1917* (Hinsdale, Ill., 1977); and John W. Chambers II, *The Tyranny of Change: America in the Progressive Era, 1900-1917* (New York, 1980). For an enriched understanding of the diversity and complexity of the contemporary scholarly quarrels about progressivism, see the essays in Lewis L. Gould, ed., *The Progressive Era* (Syracuse, N.Y., 1974), and John D. Buenker, John C. Burnham, and Robert M. Crunden, *Progressivism* (Cambridge, Mass., 1977). Most of the articles in these last two books reflect a fundamentally sympathetic—though not uncritical—opinion of progressivism.

The earliest historical treatments of progressivism also were sympathetic to reform. What they lacked was a critical distance from their subject. Among the most influential of the pioneering works were Benjamin Parke DeWitt, *The Progressive Movement* (New York, 1915); Charles A. and Mary R. Beard, *The Rise of American Civilization,* 2 vols. (New York, 1927); and Harold U. Faulkner, *The Quest for Social Justice, 1898-1914* (New York,

1931). Taking the progressives' rhetoric more or less at face value, these studies commonly failed to probe the complex motives behind reform or to scrutinize its actual results. In a somewhat similar vein were the early studies giving the agrarian interpretation of the origins of progressivism: John D. Hicks, *The Populist Revolt: A History of the Farmers' Alliance and the People's Party* (Minneapolis, Minn., 1931); Russel B. Nye, *Midwestern Progressive Politics: A Historical Study of Its Origins and Development, 1870–1950* (East Lansing, Mich., 1951); and C. Vann Woodward, *Origins of the New South, 1877–1913* (Baton Rouge, La., 1951). Woodward does, however, emphasize the racism which was inherent in southern progressivism, see, particularly, his brilliant chapter "Progressivism— For Whites Only." If the six studies noted in this paragraph were overly sympathetic to progressivism, they nonetheless gave attention to aspects of early twentieth-century reform which have been neglected too frequently in more recent works.

The initial statements of the urban, middle-class interpretation of progressivism are George Mowry, *The California Progressives* (Berkeley, Cal., 1951), and Alfred D. Chandler, Jr., "The Origins of Progressive Leadership," in Elting E. Morison, ed., *The Letters of Theodore Roosevelt,* 8 vols. (Cambridge, Mass., 1951–54), Vol. 8, pp. 1462–65. Mowry carried the interpretation forward in *The Era of Theodore Roosevelt and the Birth of Modern America, 1900–1912* (New York, 1958); but the most important expression of this viewpoint came in Richard Hofstadter, *The Age of Reform: From Bryan to F.D.R.* (New York, 1955). Although it has influenced almost all the subsequent work on progressivism, Hofstadter's book has been subjected to considerable criticism, especially for its so-called status-revolution thesis about the origins of reform. Among the studies which have criticized Hofstadter are Richard B. Sherman, "The Status Revolution and Massachusetts Progressive Leadership," *Political Science Quarterly* 78 (1963): 59–65; William T. Kerr, Jr., "The Progressives of Washington, 1910–1912," *Pacific Northwest Quarterly* 55 (1964): 16–27; E. Daniel Potts, "The Progressive Profile in Iowa," *Mid-America* 47 (1965): 257–68; and David P.

Thelen, "Social Tensions and the Origins of Progressivism," *Journal of American History* 56 (1969): 323–41. For a thoughtful recent effort to evaluate Hofstadter's argument and to suggest that his critics have by no means fully proved their case, see Jerome M. Clubb and Howard W. Allen, "Collective Biography and the Progressive Movement: The 'Status Revolution' Revisited," *Social Science History* 4 (1977): 518–34.

Revised versions of the middle-class view of progressivism, which stress the role of organized groups, dominated the literature on the subject during the 1960s and 1970s. Samuel P. Hays was perhaps the most original exponent of this interpretation, particularly in *The Response to Industrialism, 1885–1914* (Chicago, 1957) and "The Politics of Reform in Municipal Government in the Progressive Era," *Pacific Northwest Quarterly* 55 (1964): 157–69. It was Robert H. Wiebe, however, who produced the leading synthesis of the organizational interpretation: *The Search for Order, 1877–1920* (New York, 1967). Related works include Samuel Haber, *Efficiency and Uplift: Scientific Management in the Progressive Era, 1890–1920* (Chicago, 1964); Jerry Israel, ed., *Building the Organizational Society: Essays on Associational Activities in Modern America* (New York, 1972); Louis Galambos, "The Emerging Organizational Synthesis in Modern American History," *Business History Review* 44 (1970): 279–90; Louis Galambos, *The Public Image of Big Business in America, 1880–1940: A Quantitative Study in Social Change* (Baltimore, Md., 1975); and John C. Burnham, "Essay," in Buenker, Burnham, and Crunden, *Progressivism.*

Among the most important organizers of special-interest groups were businessmen. Their contributions to progressivism are evaluated in Robert H. Wiebe, *Businessmen and Reform: A Study of the Progressive Movement* (Cambridge, Mass., 1962); Gabriel Kolko, *The Triumph of Conservatism: A Reinterpretation of American History, 1900–1916* (New York, 1963); Gabriel Kolko, *Railroads and Regulation, 1877–1916* (Princeton, N.J., 1965); and James Weinstein, *The Corporate Ideal in the Liberal State, 1900–1918* (Boston, 1968). (Other studies of this subject are discussed below in connection with governmental regulation of business.)

Less organized were immigrant Americans, but their role in progressive reform is considered to have been crucial by J. Joseph Huthmacher and John D. Buenker. See in particular Huthmacher, "Urban Liberalism and the Age of Reform," *Mississippi Valley Historical Review* 49 (1962): 231–41; Huthmacher, "Charles Evans Hughes and Charles Francis Murphy: The Metamorphosis of Progressivism," *New York History* 46 (1965): 25–40; and John D. Buenker, *Urban Liberalism and Progressive Reform* (New York, 1973). Many of the works on progressivism in individual states (listed below) also treat in detail the immigrants' participation in progressivism.

Almost all the studies mentioned in the last several paragraphs have tended to emphasize one or another social source of progressivism at the expense of the rest. For four relatively recent efforts to digest and interpret the divergent views of what progressivism really was, see Thelen, "Social Tensions and the Origins of Progressivism"; John D. Buenker, "The Progressive Era: A Search for a Synthesis," *Mid-America* 51 (1969): 175–93; Peter G. Filene, "An Obituary for 'The Progressive Movement,'" *American Quarterly* 22 (1970): 20–34; and Richard L. McCormick, "The Discovery that Business Corrupts Politics: A Reappraisal of the Origins of Progressivism," *American Historical Review* 86 (1981): 247–74.

The social and economic conditions which called forth progressivism are the subjects of a literature too vast to be detailed here. Some of the key developments can be traced in Glenn Porter, *The Rise of Big Business, 1860–1910* (Arlington Heights, Ill., 1973); Melvyn Dubofsky, *Industrialism and the American Worker, 1865–1920* (Arlington Heights, Ill., 1975); and Herbert G. Gutman, *Work, Culture and Society in Industrializing America: Essays in American Working-Class and Social History* (New York, 1976). For an account of the "new immigration" of the late nineteenth and early twentieth centuries, see Alan M. Kraut, *The Huddled Masses: The Immigrant in American Society, 1860–1921* (Arlington Heights, Ill., 1982). On the social and political thought of the preprogressive years, see Richard Hofstadter, *Social Darwinism in American Thought,* rev. edn. (Boston, 1955); Sidney Fine, *Laissez-Faire and the General Welfare State: A Study of Conflict in American Thought, 1865-1901* (Ann Arbor, Mich., 1956); and R. Jackson Wilson, *In Quest of Community: Social Philosophy in the United States, 1860-1920* (New York, 1968).

The agrarian revolt which culminated in Populism during the 1890s has been the subject of considerable study—and dispute—by historians. Besides the works by Hicks, Nye, and Woodward, cited above, see especially C. Vann Woodward, *Tom Watson: Agrarian Rebel* (New York, 1938); Robert C. McMath, Jr., *Populist Vanguard: A History of the Southern Farmers' Alliance* (New York, 1975); and Lawrence Goodwyn, *Democratic Promise: The Populist Moment in America* (New York, 1976). Paul W. Glad's *McKinley, Bryan, and the People* (Philadelphia, 1964) provides a brief, lively narrative of the political crisis of the 1890s, while three more recent studies analyze the electoral realignment which occurred during that decade: Paul Kleppner, *The Cross of Culture: A Social Analysis of Midwestern Politics, 1850-1900* (New York, 1970); Richard J. Jensen, *The Winning of the Midwest: Social and Political Conflict, 1888-1896* (New York, 1971); and Samuel T. McSeveney, *The Politics of Depression: Political Behavior in the Northeast, 1893-1896* (New York, 1972).

The crystallization of progressive thought in the aftermath of the 1890s has been treated in a number of major books. Eric F. Goldman's *Rendezvous With Destiny: A History of Modern American Reform* (New York, 1952) emphasizes how reforming intellectuals broke the "steel chain" of conservative ideas, while Morton White's *Social Thought in America: The Revolt Against Formalism* (New York, 1949) stresses the way that thinkers rejected the rigid categories of the nineteenth-century mind. A third overview of progressive thought may be found in David W. Noble, *The Progressive Mind, 1890-1917* (Chicago, 1970). For a study of the ideas of three seminal reformers, see Charles Forcey, *The Crossroads of Liberalism: Croly, Weyl, Lippmann, and the Progressive Era, 1900-1925* (New York, 1961). The communitarian components of progressive thought are treated in Wilson, *In Quest of Community,* and in Jean B. Quandt, *From the Small Town to the Great Community: The Social Thought of Progressive Intellectuals* (New Brunswick, N.J., 1970). Finally, for a thoughtful and imaginative interpretation of the way in which progressives looked at the world, see Clyde Griffen, "The Progressive Ethos," in Stanley Coben and Lorman Ratner, eds., *The Development of an American Culture* (Englewood Cliffs, N.J., 1970), pp. 120–49.

The writings of the muckrakers ought to be read in their original form by anyone interested in understanding the ideas and passions which lay behind early twentieth-century reform. A representative selection of muckraking journalism may be found in Arthur and Lila Weinberg, eds., *The Muckrakers: The Era in Journalism that Moved America to Reform—The Most Significant Magazine Articles of 1902-1912* (New York, 1961). Louis Filler's study, *The Muckrakers: Crusaders for American Liberalism* (University Park, Pa., 1976), remains the best overall narrative on the subject. Among the more specialized works are David M. Chalmers, *The Social and Political Ideas of the Muckrakers* (New York, 1964); Peter Lyon, *Success Story: The Life and Times of S. S. McClure* (New York, 1963); and Justin Kaplan, *Lincoln Steffens: A Biography* (New York, 1974). The most brilliant single account ever given of muckraking is Part III of *The Autobiography of Lincoln Steffens* (New York, 1931). Carefully (and somewhat self-servingly) written years afterward, Steffens' account nonetheless gives us an enormously insightful interpretation of the shocks and discoveries which generated the popular dynamics of progressivism.

Early twentieth-century reform came first to the cities, and many historians have treated progressivism essentially as a movement which flowed outward from urban America. Two of the most interesting, although not wholly convincing, interpretations of the reform impulse in the cities may be found in the works of Samuel P. Hays and Melvin G. Holli. See especially Hays' article "The Politics of Reform in Municipal Government in the Progressive Era"; Holli, *Reform in Detroit: Hazen S. Pingree and Urban Politics* (New York, 1969); and Holli, "Urban Reform in the Progressive Era," in Gould, ed., *The Progressive*

Era, pp. 133–51. Martin J. Schiesl's fine recent book, *The Politics of Efficiency: Municipal Administration and Reform in America, 1880–1920* (Berkeley, Cal., 1977), builds on—but also revises—the work of both Hays and Holli. On progressive city commissions, see Bradley R. Rice, *Progressive Cities: The Commission Government Movement in America, 1901–1920* (Austin, Tex., 1977). For some of the most notable studies of reform in particular cities, see James B. Crooks, *Politics and Progress: The Rise of Urban Progressivism in Baltimore, 1895 to 1911* (Baton Rouge, La., 1968); Zane L. Miller, *Boss Cox's Cincinnati: Urban Politics in the Progressive Era* (New York, 1968); Carl V. Harris, *Political Power in Birmingham, 1871–1921* (Knoxville, Tenn., 1977); David C. Hammack, *Power and Society: Greater New York at the Turn of the Century* (New York, 1982); Walton Bean, *Boss Ruef's San Francisco: The Story of the Union Labor Party, Big Business, and the Graft Prosecution* (Berkeley, Cal., 1952); and Eugene M. Tobin, "The Commission Plan in Jersey City, 1911–1917: The Ambiguity of Municipal Reform in the Progressive Era," in Joel Schwartz and Daniel Prosser, eds., *Cities of the Garden State: Essays in the Urban and Suburban History of New Jersey* (Dubuque, Iowa, 1977), pp. 71–84.

While progressivism everywhere shared some basic characteristics, historians have long recognized regional differences in the origins and the nature of reform. On southern progressivism, see Arthur S. Link, "The Progressive Movement in the South, 1870–1914," *North Carolina Historical Review* 23 (1946): 172–95; Woodward, *Origins of the New South;* Jack Temple Kirby, *Darkness at the Dawning: Race and Reform in the Progressive South* (Philadelphia, 1972); and Dewey W. Grantham, Jr., "The Contours of Southern Progressivism," *American Historical Review* 86 (1981): 1035–59. For a regional study of midwestern reform, consult Nye, *Midwestern Progressive Politics.* There are, unfortunately, no comparable historical works on progressivism in the East or the Far West.

State progressivism has, however, been a fertile field for

study, with most individual states the subject of at least one book-length work. Three widely scattered states—Wisconsin, California, and New York—have inspired an outpouring of books. A traditional pro-progressive view of affairs in Wisconsin is Robert S. Maxwell, *La Follette and the Rise of Progressives in Wisconsin* (Madison, Wisc., 1956), while more critical, revisionist viewpoints are offered in Herbert F. Margulies, *The Decline of the Progressive Movement in Wisconsin, 1890–1920* (Madison, Wisc., 1968); David P. Thelen, *The New Citizenship: Origins of Progressivism in Wisconsin, 1885–1900* (Columbia, Mo., 1972); and Stanley P. Caine, *The Myth of a Progressive Reform: Railroad Regulation in Wisconsin, 1903–1910* (Madison, Wisc., 1970). Mowry's *The California Progressives* gave the first detailed analysis of reform in that state, while, more recently, Spencer C. Olin, Jr., *California's Prodigal Sons: Hiram Johnson and the Progressives, 1911–1917* (Berkeley, Cal., 1968), and Mansel G. Blackford, *The Politics of Business in California, 1890–1920* (Columbus, Ohio, 1977), have offered revised understandings of progressivism in California. Political progressivism in New York has been treated in three books: G. Wallace Chessman, *Governor Theodore Roosevelt: The Albany Apprenticeship, 1898–1900* (Cambridge, Mass., 1965); Robert F. Wesser, *Charles Evans Hughes: Politics and Reform in New York, 1905–1910* (Ithaca, N.Y., 1967); and Richard L. McCormick, *From Realignment to Reform: Political Change in New York State, 1893–1910* (Ithaca, N.Y., 1981). For more specialized aspects of reform in the Empire State, see Irwin Yellowitz, *Labor and the Progressive Movement in New York State, 1897–1916* (Ithaca, N.Y., 1967); Jeremy P. Felt, *Hostages of Fortune: Child Labor Reform in New York State* (Syracuse, N.Y., 1965); Roy Lubove, *The Progressives and the Slums: Tenement House Reform in New York City, 1890–1917* (Pittsburgh, Pa., 1962); and Melvyn Dubofsky, *When Workers Organize: New York City in the Progressive Era* (Amherst, Mass., 1968.).

Besides the works on Wisconsin, California, and New

York, there are numerous other notable studies of state progressivism. On the South, see Sheldon Hackney, *Populism to Progressivism in Alabama* (Princeton, N.J., 1969); Raymond H. Pulley, *Old Virginia Restored: An Interpretation of the Progressive Impulse, 1870–1930* (Charlottesville, Va., 1968); Dewey W. Grantham, Jr., *Hoke Smith and the Politics of the New South* (Baton Rouge, La., 1958) [a study of progressivism in Georgia]; William F. Holmes, *The White Chief: James Kimble Vardaman* (Baton Rouge, La., 1970) [Mississippi]; and Lewis L. Gould, *Progressives and Prohibitionists: Texas Democrats in the Wilson Era* (Austin, Tex., 1973). For state progressivism in the Midwest, see Hoyt Landon Warner, *Progressivism in Ohio, 1897–1917* (Columbus, Ohio, 1964); Robert W. Cherny, *Populism, Progressivism, and the Transformation of Nebraska Politics, 1885–1915* (Lincoln, Neb., 1981); Robert S. La Forte, *Leaders of Reform: Progressive Republicans in Kansas, 1900–1916* (Lawrence, Kan., 1974); and Charles N. Glaab, "The Failure of North Dakota Progressivism," *Mid-America* 39 (1957): 195–209. Among the most interesting studies of progressivism in the eastern states are Ransom E. Noble, Jr., *New Jersey Progressivism Before Wilson* (Princeton, N.J., 1946); Winston Allen Flint, *The Progressive Movement in Vermont* (Washington, D.C., 1941); and Richard M. Abrams, *Conservatism in a Progressive Era: Massachusetts Politics, 1900–1912* (Cambridge, Mass., 1964). Early twentieth-century voting behavior has not received sufficient attention from historians, but two states, at least, have been studied: Roger E. Wyman, "Middle-Class Voters and Progressive Reform: The Conflicts of Class and Culture," *American Political Science Review* 69 (1974): 488–504 [Wisconsin], and Michael Paul Rogin and John L. Shover, *Political Change in California: Critical Elections and Social Movements, 1890–1966* (Westport, Conn., 1970), Chaps. 2 and 3.

There are many histories of national politics during the progressive era. Mowry's *The Era of Theodore Roosevelt* and Arthur S. Link's *Woodrow Wilson and the Progressive Era, 1910–1917,* rev. edn. (New York, 1963) together provide a comprehensive survey of the period 1901 to 1917. Lewis L. Gould's *Reform and Regulation: American Politics, 1900–1916* (New York, 1978) offers a briefer, interpretive account of national affairs. On the leading Democrats and their divisions, see J. Rogers Hollingsworth, *The Whirligig of Politics: The Democracy of Cleveland and Bryan* (New York, 1963); and for studies of the top Republicans, consult Horace S. and Marion G. Merrill, *The Republican Command, 1897–1913* (Lexington, Ky., 1971), and Nathaniel W. Stephenson, *Nelson W. Aldrich: A Leader in American Politics* (New York, 1930). Theodore Roosevelt has been the subject of innumerable books; among the best are John M. Blum, *The Republican Roosevelt* (Cambridge, Mass., 1954); William H. Harbaugh, *The Life and Times of Theodore Roosevelt,* rev. edn. (New York, 1975); and Edmund Morris, *The Rise of Theodore Roosevelt* (New York, 1979). For divergent accounts of natural-resource conservation, see J. Leonard Bates, "Fulfilling American Democracy: The Conservation Movement, 1907 to 1921," *Mississippi Valley Historical Review* 44 (1957): 29–57, and *The Origins of Teapot Dome: Progressives, Parties, and Petroleum, 1909–1921* (Urbana, Ill., 1963); and Samuel P. Hays, *Conservation and the Gospel of Efficiency: The Progressive Conservation Movement, 1890–1920* (Cambridge, Mass., 1959).

Historians, on the whole, have treated kindly the insurgent Republicans who quarreled with Roosevelt's successor, William Howard Taft. The lives of two of them may be traced in John Braeman, *Albert J. Beveridge: American Nationalist* (Chicago, 1971), and Belle C. and Fola La Follette, *Robert M. La Follette,* 2 vols. (New York, 1953). Their revolt against the regular party leadership is the subject of James Holt, *Congressional Insurgents and the Party System, 1909–1916* (Cambridge, Mass., 1967). Taft's troubled presidency has been studied in Donald F. Anderson, *William Howard Taft: A Conservative's Conception of the Presidency* (Ithaca, N.Y., 1973), and Norman M. Wilensky, *Conservatives in the Progressive Era: The Taft Republicans of 1912* (Gainesville, Fla., 1965). On the Socialist party, which reached its peak of influence during the Taft years, see David A. Shannon, *The Socialist Party of America: A History* (New York, 1955); James Weinstein, *The Decline of Socialism in America, 1912–1925* (New York, 1967); Ray Ginger, *The Bending Cross: A Biography of Eugene Victor Debs* (New Brunswick, N.J., 1949); and James R. Green, *Grass-Roots Socialism: Radical Movements in the Southwest, 1895–1943* (Baton Rouge, La., 1978).

Arthur S. Link's *Wilson*, 5 vols. (Princeton, N.J., 1947-65) is the indispensable study of its subject. *Wilson: The Road to the White House* (1947) chronicles Wilson's life through his election to the presidency in 1912, while the subsequent volumes published to date cover his administration from 1913 to 1917. A paper by Allan J. Lichtman and Jack B. Lord II, "Party Loyalty and Progressive Politics: Quantitative Analysis of the Vote for President in 1912," Organization of American Historians Annual Meeting, April 1979, provides a fresh look at the results of the election of 1912.

A number of historians and political scientists have attempted to give overall interpretations of the political and governmental transformation accomplished during the progressive era. Among the most interesting books are several which focus on changing patterns of public policy: James Willard Hurst, *Law and the Conditions of Freedom in the Nineteenth-Century United States* (Madison, Wisc., 1956), Chap. 3; Grant McConnell, *Private Power and American Democracy* (New York, 1966), Chap. 2; and Theodore J. Lowi, *The End of Liberalism: Ideology, Policy, and the Crisis of Public Authority* (New York, 1969), Chaps. 1–3. For a pathbreaking study of new patterns of voting behavior, see Walter Dean Burnham, "The Changing Shape of the American Political Universe," *American Political Science Review* 59 (1965): 7–28. On the changes through which political parties went in this era, consult Samuel P. Hays, "Political Parties and the Community-Society Continuum," in William Nisbet Chambers and Walter Dean Burnham, eds., *The American Party Systems: Stages of Political Development* (New York, 1967), pp. 152–81, and Robert D. Marcus, *Grand Old Party: Political Structure in the*

Gilded Age, 1880–1896 (New York, 1971), Chap. 8. Another recent interpretive account of political and governmental innovations is McCormick, "The Discovery that Business Corrupts Politics."

Several older works which treat the election-law reforms of the progressive era include Charles Edward Merriam and Louise Overacker, *Primary Elections* (Chicago, 1928); Earl R. Sikes, *State and Federal Corrupt-Practices Legislation* (Durham, N.C., 1928); Louise Overacker, *Money in Elections* (New York, 1932); and Joseph P. Harris, *Election Administration in the United States* (Washington, D.C., 1934). Modern interpretations of these reforms date from the publication of V. O. Key, Jr.'s *American State Politics: An Introduction* (New York, 1956), which includes a brilliant account of the direct primary and its effects. For recent understandings of the election-law changes of the late 1800s and early 1900s, together with efforts to estimate their impact on voting behavior, see Jerrold G. Rusk, "The Effect of the Australian Ballot Reform on Split Ticket Voting, 1876–1908," *American Political Science Review* 64 (1970): 1220–38; Peter H. Argersinger, "'A Place on the Ballot': Fusion Politics and Antifusion Laws," *American Historical Review* 85 (1980): 287–306; Paul Kleppner and Stephen C. Baker, "The Impact of Voter Registration Requirements on Electoral Turnout, 1900–16," *Journal of Political and Military Sociology* 8 (1980): 205–26; and Lloyd Sponholtz, "The Initiative and Referendum: Direct Democracy in Perspective, 1898–1920," *American Studies* 14 (1973): 43–64. John Reynolds, "'The Silent Dollar': Vote Buying in New Jersey," *New Jersey History* 98 (1980): 191–211, chronicles the progressive assault on the common nineteenth-century practice of purchasing votes.

Woman suffrage, the most important single electoral reform of the progressive era, has been the subject of numerous studies. See especially Eleanor Flexner, *Century of Struggle: The Woman's Rights Movement in the United States* (Cambridge, Mass., 1959); Aileen S. Kraditor, *The Ideas of the Woman Suffrage Movement, 1890–1920* (New York, 1965); and Christine Lunardini, "From Equal Suffrage to Equal Rights: The National

Woman's Party, 1913–1923," Ph.D. dissertation, Princeton University, 1981. For an excellent account of the radical implications of suffrage, see Ellen Carol DuBois, *Feminism and Suffrage: The Emergence of an Independent Women's Movement in America, 1848–1869* (Ithaca, N.Y., 1978).

The exclusion of southern blacks from the electorate in the 1890s and early 1900s was considered by many progressives to be just as necessary a "reform" as were the other election-law changes of the era. The best starting point for the study of disfranchisement is C. Vann Woodward's seminal study, *The Strange Career of Jim Crow*, rev. 3rd edn. (New York, 1974). Another interpretation of the subject and of the relationship between disfranchisement and progressivism may be found in Kirby, *Darkness at the Dawning*. Sheldon Hackney's *Populism to Progressivism in Alabama* includes a careful treatment of one state's decision to exclude blacks from the polls. The best and most comprehensive study of this subject is J. Morgan Kousser's work, *The Shaping of Southern Politics: Suffrage Restriction and the Establishment of the One-Party South, 1880–1910* (New Haven, Conn., 1974). Based on a sophisticated quantitative analysis, Kousser's book shows that wealthy southern Democrats sought to achieve both economic and partisan goals through disfranchisement and that they succeeded.

The best introduction to the rise of special-interest groups in this period is Hays, *The Response to Industrialism*. Many of the city and state studies cited above also treat this subject. See particularly Harris, *Political Power in Birmingham*; Margulies, *The Decline of the Progressive Movement in Wisconsin*; Caine, *The Myth of a Progressive Reform*; Blackford, *The Politics of Business in California*; and McCormick, *From Realignment to Reform*.

Thomas K. McCraw has provided an excellent survey of the literature on the regulation of business in "Regulation in America: A Review Article," *Business History Review* 49 (1975): 159–83. For the traditional interpretation, which suggested that regulation was intended solely to assist the "people" against the business interests, see Harold U. Faulkner, *The Decline of Laissez Faire, 1897–1917* (New York, 1951). Gabriel Kolko completely inverted this point of view in *Railroads and Regulation* and *The Triumph of Conservatism*. While his work has been influential, Kolko has not gone unchallenged. For a convincing reversal of his account of the effects of railroad regulation, see Albro Martin, *Enterprise Denied: Origins of the Decline of American Railroads, 1897–1917* (New York, 1971). An article by Alan L. Seltzer, "Woodrow Wilson as a 'Corporate Liberal': Toward a Reconsideration of Left Revisionist Historiography," *Western Political Quarterly* 30 (1977): 183–212, rejects Kolko's interpretation of Wilson's relationship to large corporate interests. William Graebner, *Coal-Mining Safety in the Progressive Period: The Political Economy of Reform* (Lexington, Ky., 1976), and H. Roger Grant, *Insurance Reform: Consumer Action in the Progressive Era* (Ames, Iowa, 1979), are studies of the regulation of particular industries. John Braeman has provided a careful account of the adoption of one key federal regulatory measure, the Meat Inspection Act of 1906, in his article "The Square Deal in Action: A Case Study in the Growth of the 'National Police Power'," in John Braeman, Robert H. Bremner, and Everett Walters, eds., *Change and Continuity in Twentieth-Century America* (Columbus, Ohio, 1964), pp. 35–80. Several scholars have written about the Food and Drug Act which also was passed in 1906: James Harvey Young, *The Toadstool Millionaires: A Social History of Patent Medicines in America before Federal Regulation* (Princeton, N.J., 1961); Sarah Stage, *Female Complaints: Lydia Pinkham and the Business of Women's Medicine* (New York, 1979); and Peter Temin, *Taking Your Medicine: Drug Regulation in the United States* (Cambridge, Mass., 1980). The best state-level study of business regulation is Caine, *The Myth of a Progressive Reform*.

Elizabeth Brandeis, "Labor Legislation," in John R. Commons et al., eds., *History of Labour in the United States*, 4 vols. (New York, 1918–1935), Vol. 3, pp. 399–697, remains the best overview of social reform in the progressive era. Still valuable also is Harold U. Faulkner's *The Quest for Social Justice*. While the latter's interpretation is out of date, the book contains a full narrative of the era's leading social and cultural developments. For the most part, the various movements for justice and control must be studied in a diversity of books and articles, many of which are excellent. One useful starting point is Gerald N. Grob's "The Political System and Social Policy in the Nineteenth Century: Legacy of the Revolution," *Mid-America* 58 (1976): 5–19, which gives an interpretive account of the nineteenth-century patterns of social policy from which the progressives departed. For a discussion of social justice and social control, see Don S. Kirshner, "The Ambiguous Legacy: Social Justice and Social Control in the Progressive Era," *Historical Reflections* 2 (1975): 69–88.

The fullest account of the settlement-house movement is Allen F. Davis' sympathetic study, *Spearheads for Reform: The Social Settlements and the Progressive Movement, 1890–1914* (New York, 1967). For a more critical treatment of the settlement workers and their philanthropic supporters, see John F. McClymer, *War and Welfare: Social Engineering in America, 1890–1925* (Westport, Conn., 1980). The social work profession that sprang from settlement work is studied in Roy Lubove, *The Professional Altruist: The Emergence of Social Work as a Career, 1880–1930* (Cambridge, Mass., 1965), and James Leiby, *A History of Social Welfare and Social Work in the United States* (New York, 1978).

Background on the condition of women in the early twentieth century may be found in William L. O'Neill, *Divorce in the Progressive Era* (New Haven, Conn., 1967); Lois W. Banner, *Women in Modern America: A Brief History* (New York, 1974); and Carl N. Degler, *At Odds: Women and the Family in America from the Revolution to the Present* (New York, 1980). No one interested in progressivism should neglect Jane Addams' classic *Twenty Years at Hull-House* (New York, 1910). For a provocative account of her life, see Allen F. Davis, *American Heroine: The Life and Legend of Jane Addams* (New York, 1973). Other interpretive treatments of women reformers include William L. O'Neill, *Everyone Was Brave: The Rise and Fall of Feminism in America* (Chicago, 1969), and Jill Conway, "Women Reformers and American Culture, 1870–1930," *Journal of Social History* 5 (1971–72): 164–77. On the progressives' assault on prostitution, see Roy Lubove, "The Progressives and the Prostitute," *Historian* 24 (1962): 308–30, and Mark Thomas Connelly, *The Response to Prostitution in the Progressive Era* (Chapel Hill, N.C., 1980).

For an excellent introduction to the conditions of workers and to the patterns of working-class protest in the early 1900s, see David Brody, "The American Worker in the Progressive Age: A Comprehensive Analysis," in Brody, *Workers in Industrial America: Essays on the Twentieth Century Struggle* (New York, 1980), pp. 3–47. An earlier study by Brody, *Steelworkers in America: The Nonunion Era* (Cambridge, Mass., 1960), is a superb analysis of workers' lives in one industry. Melvyn Dubofsky's two books, cited above, treat respectively the workers of a single city and the general relationship between labor and progressivism: *When Workers Organize* and *Industrialism and the American Worker*. See also Yellowitz, *Labor and the Progressive Movement in New York State*, and Felt, *Hostages of Fortune*.

Robert H. Bremner's pathbreaking book, *From the Depths: The Discovery of Poverty in the United States* (New York, 1956), recounts the development of an environmental interpretation of urban poverty. Roy Lubove's *The Progressives and the Slums* treats housing reform in a single city, while Dominick Cavallo, *Muscles and Morals: Organized Playgrounds and Urban Reform, 1880–1920* (Philadelphia, 1981), analyzes the progressive movement for improved urban recreational facilities. Paul Boyer's *Urban Masses and Moral Order in America, 1820–1920* (Cambridge, Mass., 1978) emphasizes that social control was an important progressive objective and places early twentieth-century urban reform squarely in the context of a tradition which dated back to the Jacksonian period.

The best introduction to the reforming professionals of the progressive era is Robert H. Wiebe's seminal chapter, "A New

Middle Class," in *The Search for Order*. For two dissents from Wiebe's overall interpretation of this group's influence, see Wayne K. Hobson, "Professionals, Progressives, and Bureaucratization: A Reassessment," *Historian* 39 (1977), 639–58; and McClymer, *War and Welfare*. Several brilliant articles by John C. Burnham treat the work of the era's reforming physicians: "Medical Specialists and Movements Toward Social Control in the Progressive Era: Three Examples," in Israel, ed., *Building the Organizational Society,* pp. 19–30; "The Progressive Era Revolution in American Attitudes Toward Sex," *Journal of American History* 59 (1973): 885–908; and "Essay," in Burnham, Buenker, and Crunden, eds., *Progressivism*. Other valuable studies of the medical profession include Gerald E. Markowitz and David Rosner, "Doctors in Crisis: Medical Education and Medical Reform During the Progressive Era, 1895–1915," in Susan Reverby and David Rosner, eds., *Health Care in America: Essays in Social History* (Philadelphia, 1979), pp. 185–205, and Morris J. Vogel, *The Invention of the Modern Hospital: Boston, 1870–1930* (Chicago, 1980). Progressive psychiatrists and their reforms have been the subjects of several works which include Barbara Sicherman, "The Quest for Mental Health in America, 1880–1917," Ph.D. dissertation, Columbia University, 1967; and David J. Rothman, *Conscience and Convenience: The Asylum and its Alternatives in Progressive America* (Boston, 1980). We have also benefited from reading Gerald N. Grob's forthcoming book, *Institutional Care in Modern America* (Princeton, N.J., 1983).

The basic works on progressive education and educators are Lawrence A. Cremin, *The Transformation of the School: Progressivism in American Education, 1876–1957* (New York, 1971), and Rush Welter, *Popular Education and Democratic Thought in America* (New York, 1962). David B. Tyack, "City Schools: Centralization of Control at the Turn of the Century," in Israel, ed., *Building the Organizational Society,* pp. 57–72, and his *The One Best System: A History of American Urban Education* (Cambridge, Mass., 1974) discuss the centralization of urban school systems, while Raymond Callahan, *Education and the Cult of Efficiency* (Chicago, 1962), describes the application of business efficiency to the tasks of education. On the new mental testing of the progressive era, see Mark H. Haller, *Eugenics: Hereditarian Attitudes in American Thought* (New Brunswick, N.J., 1963). For the drive to improve the schools of the South, consult Woodward, *Origins of the New South,* Chaps. 15 and 16; Kirby, *Darkness at the Dawning,* Chap. 5; and William A. Link, "Public Schooling and Social Change in Rural Virginia, 1870–1920," Ph.D. dissertation, University of Virginia, 1981. Two other groups of reforming professionals are studied in Samuel Walker, *Popular Justice: A History of American Criminal Justice* (New York, 1980), Chap. 6; William L. Bowers, *The Country Life Movement in America, 1900–1920* (Port Washington, N.Y., 1974); and David B. Danbom, *The Resisted Revolution: Urban America and the Industrialization of Agriculture, 1900–1930* (Ames, Iowa, 1979).

The more coercive social reforms of the progressive era have not received as much attention as they merit. In the case of most of these crusades, the exact relationships between rhetoric, intentions, and achievements remain obscure. Still, there are some extremely valuable historical studies. On racial segregation in the South, see Woodward, *The Strange Career of Jim Crow;* Hackney, *Populism to Progressivism in Alabama;* and Kirby, *Darkness at the Dawning.* On segregation in the federal bureaucracy, see August Meier, "The Rise of Segregation in the Federal Bureaucracy, 1900–1930," *Phylon* 28 (1967): 178–84. The most profound interpretive study of how black intellectuals responded to the intense racism of the era is August Meier, *Negro Thought in America, 1880–1915: Racial Ideologies in the Age of Booker T. Washington* (Ann Arbor, Mich., 1963). A recent account, which studies the racial thought of one leading progressive politician, is Thomas G. Dyer, *Theodore Roosevelt and the Idea of Race* (Baton Rouge, La., 1980).

For the response of native-born Americans to immigrants of the era, see John Higham, *Strangers in the Land: Patterns of American Nativism, 1860–1925* (New Brunswick, N.J., 1955). A more specialized study of this same topic is Roger Daniels, *The*

Politics of Prejudice: The Anti-Japanese Movement in California and the Struggle for Japanese Exclusion (Berkeley, Cal., 1962). Other aspects of nativism, including the movement for Americanization, are treated in Buenker, *Urban Liberalism and Progressive Reform;* Boyer, *Urban Masses and Moral Order;* and McClymer, *War and Welfare.* The prohibition of alcoholic beverages, a progressive reform with explicit ethnic and cultural overtones, may be studied in the following works: James H. Timberlake, *Prohibition and the Progressive Movement, 1900–1920* (Cambridge, Mass., 1963); Joseph R. Gusfield, *Symbolic Crusade: Status Politics and the American Temperance Movement* (Urbana, Ill., 1963); and Norman H. Clark, *Deliver Us From Evil: An Interpretation of American Prohibition* (New York, 1976).

The foreign policy of the progressive era is not treated in this book. For detailed bibliographies on the subjects of American overseas expansion and the coming of the First World War, see Leary and Link, eds., *The Progressive Era and the Great War.* The relationships between domestic reform and international relations are discussed in John M. Cooper, Jr., "Progressivism and American Foreign Policy: A Reconsideration," *Mid-America* 51 (1969): 260–77. Link's multivolume biography of Wilson, cited above, provides the most detailed narrative of prewar foreign relations, while the same author's *Woodrow Wilson: Revolution, War, and Peace* (Arlington Heights, Ill., 1979) gives a compact, interpretive assessment of Wilson's international role. An important series of essays is Arthur S. Link, ed., *Woodrow Wilson and a Revolutionary World, 1913–1921* (Chapel Hill, N.C., 1982). For a different understanding of Wilson's foreign policy, see N. Gordon Levin, Jr., *Woodrow Wilson and World Politics: America's Response to War and Revolution* (New York, 1968). On the beginnings of American involvement in the First World War, see John M. Cooper, Jr., *The Vanity of Power: American Isolationism and the First World War, 1914–1917* (Westport, Conn., 1969). The peace progressives, including the more conservative types as well as the genuine pacifists, are treated in C. Roland

Marchand, *The American Peace Movement and Social Reform, 1898–1918* (Princeton, N.J., 1972) and Charles DeBenedetti, *The Peace Reform in American History* (Bloomington, Ind., 1980). On social reformers and intellectuals during the war, see Allen F. Davis, "Welfare, Reform, and World War I," *American Quarterly* 19 (1967): 516–33, and William E. Leuchtenburg, "The New Deal and the Analogue of War," in Braeman et al., eds., *Change and Continuity in Twentieth-Century America*, pp. 81–143. For a recent overview of the home front, see David M. Kennedy, *Over Here: The First World War and American Society* (New York, 1980). More detailed accounts of particular aspects of wartime life may be found in numerous studies. On the federal government's control of industry, see Robert D. Cuff, *The War Industries Board: Business-Government Relations during World War I* (Baltimore, 1973); and for an account of how one group of progressive experts worked its will on the military, see Daniel J. Kevles, "Testing the Army's Intelligence: Psychologists and the Military in World War I," *Journal of American History* 55 (1968): 565–81. The wartime experiences of immigrant Americans are the subject of Frederick C. Luebke, *Bonds of Loyalty: German Americans and World War I* (DeKalb, Ill., 1976); while McClymer's *War and Welfare* describes the drive to Americanize the immigrants during the war. Zechariah Chafee, Jr., *Free Speech in the United States* (Cambridge, Mass., 1941), although flawed, remains the most detailed account of the fate of civil liberties during the World War. For a balanced specialized study of that subject, see Donald D. Johnson, *The Challenge to American Freedom: World War I and the Rise of the American Civil Liberties Union* (Lexington, Ky., 1963). H. C. Peterson and Gilbert C. Fite, *Opponents of War, 1917–1918* (Madison, Wisc., 1957), provides an account of the resistance to the war effort among radicals, Socialists, and agrarians.

Historians have given divergent assessments of the waning of progressivism and of the extent to which its achievements persisted into the 1920s and beyond. Most would agree that the years following the First World War brought a change in the national mood; for two accounts of the fear and violence of that era, see Robert K. Murray, *Red Scare: A Study in National Hysteria, 1919-1920* (New York, 1955), and Stanley Coben, "A Study in Nativism: The American Red Scare of 1919-1920," *Political Science Quarterly* 79 (1964): 52-75. On the transformation of the Democratic party, consult David Burner, *The Politics of Provincialism: The Democratic Party in Transition, 1918-1932* (New York, 1968); and for an account of the fading of the Socialists, see Weinstein, *The Decline of Socialism in America.*

George B. Tindall, *The Emergence of the New South, 1913-1945* (Baton Rouge, La., 1967), is the only work which chronicles the continued expansion of progressive programs in the states in the 1920s. Arthur S. Link's article, "What Happened to the Progressive Movement in the 1920's?" *American Historical Review* 64 (1959): 833-51, makes the case that much of progressivism endured into the 1920s, while Paul Glad's essay, "Progressives and the Business Culture of the 1920s," *Journal of American History* 53 (1966): 75-89, develops a similar argument about a more specialized aspect of the subject. For contrary accounts of progressivism's relationship to the New Deal, see Otis L. Graham, Jr., *An Encore for Reform: The Old Progressives and the New Deal* (New York, 1967), and Andrew M. Scott, "The Progressive Era in Perspective," *Journal of Politics* 21 (1959): 685-701. Finally, for two assessments of progressivism as a whole, see Richard Abrams, "The Failure of Progressivism," in Richard Abrams and Lawrence Levine, eds., *The Shaping of Twentieth Century America* (Boston, 1971), pp. 207-24, which takes a critical view, and Thomas McCraw, "The Legacy of the Progressive Era," in Gould, ed., *The Progressive Era,* pp. 181-202, which renders a more favorable judgment.

INDEX

Addams, Jane, 73, 74, 100
administrative government, 32, 36–37, 57
  progressives' attitudes toward, 61–62, 116
agricultural credits, 18, 47, 94, 112
agricultural extension, 47, 94
Agriculture Department, 64
Alabama, 32
alcoholism, 68, 74, 79, 102
  See also prohibition of alcoholic beverages
American City Planning Institute, 93
American Federation of Labor, 14, 27, 56
  cooperation of with the Democratic party, 40, 42, 56
"Americanization," 100–101
American Medical Association, 86
American Red Cross, 107
American Tobacco Company, 37
Amherst College, 73
Andover House, 77
Anti-Saloon League, 103
antisepsis, 86

Argersinger, Peter, 51
asepsis, 86
Australian ballot, 50–51

Baker, Ray Stannard, 24
Baker, Stephen, 55
banking corporations, 4, 46
Banner, Lois W., 75
Beard, Charles A., 4
Beard, Mary R., 4
Beef Trust, 37
Beers, Clifford, 88
Berger, Victor L., 40
Binet, Alfred, 92
blacks
  education of, 90–91
  exclusion of from voting, 33–34, 53, 96
  literacy of, 91
  segregation of, 33, 96–99
Blaine, James G., 14
Bolshevik Revolution, 109
Boston, Massachusetts, 77
Bourne, Randolph, 106
Bowers, William L., 93–94